THE
IRRESISTIBLE
CHURCH

WAYNE CORDEIRO

THE
IRRESISTIBLE
CHURCH

BETHANYHOUSE
Minneapolis, Minnesota

Published by Bethany House Publishers
11400 Hampshire Avenue South
Bloomington, Minnesota 55438

Bethany House Publishers is a division of
Baker Publishing Group, Grand Rapids, Michigan.

Printed in the United States of America

In keeping with biblical principles of creation stewardship, Baker Publishing Group advocates the responsible use of our natural resources. As a member of the Green Press Initiative, our company uses recycled paper when possible. The text paper of this book is comprised of 30% post-consumer waste.

Library of Congress Cataloging-in-Publication Data

Cordeiro, Wayne.
    The irresistible church : 12 traits of a church heaven applauds / Wayne Cordeiro ; fore-
word by Bill Hybels.
        p.   cm.
    Summary: "A successful pastor and church planter reveals twelve keys to church growth—
qualities that can make any church one that people love to be a part of and God can't help
but bless"—Provided by publisher.
    Includes bibliographical references (p.   ).
    ISBN 978-0-7642-0885-0 (hardcover : alk. paper) 1. Church growth. 2. Church
attendance. I. Title.
    BV652.25.C67   2011
    254'.5—dc22

2011002919

This book is dedicated to two brides:

One is my dear wife, Anna, who for more than thirty-five years has always reminded me that it is only through love that lives are changed—mine included.

The other is the bride of Christ, the church . . . one expression in particular, New Hope Oahu— a network of radiant and joyful servants who embody the definition of grace and beauty in the islands of Hawaii.

Books by
Wayne Cordeiro

The Divine Mentor

Leading on Empty

The Irresistible Church

CONTENTS

FOREWORD

I've always been captivated by the vision of what a church can be—an authentic community of faith that reaches increasing numbers of lost people and helps them grow into fully devoted followers of Jesus Christ.

Yet sometimes churches do not reach their full redemptive potential. They motor along year after year, well entrenched in programs and traditions, but ineffective in their main calling.

My hope is that churches across the world will make regular, strategic adjustments toward finding and following our true calling of reaching people with the gospel. Any time we can become more effective in this task it is well worth the effort.

Think of this book as a strategic tool. The big idea of this book is *not* that we need to shine ourselves up in order to receive Christ's blessing, but rather that we will adjust our course to follow the whispers of His leading. We want to become churches that people love to attend and that God uses to advance His kingdom. We want to live the words of 2 Corinthians 5:9, both individually and as churches: "We make it our goal to please him."

Why are the concepts presented in this book so important? The older I get, the more aware I am that I only have this day until my final day to get the word of Christ out to as many people as possible. Since the day I became a Christian on a Wisconsin hillside, when I was seventeen, I've wanted everyone I meet to experience the saving grace found in Jesus Christ. My aim is to rid myself of life's superfluous activities and take the transforming message of saving grace to everyone I'm able. As my days get fewer, my sense of urgency for the sake of the kingdom is going up, not down.

I believe that through Jesus Christ, the church is the hope of the world, and we as Christians need not make any apologies for wanting to get better at what we are called to do. We must be dead serious about helping people come to know Christ and about helping Christians grow to be Christ centered.

No matter whether you're a pastor, a layleader, or a congregant, this book contains well-proven principles that when applied will become breakthrough ideas to take your church to the next level of effectiveness.

—Bill Hybels, senior pastor
Willow Creek Community Church

INTRODUCTION

GETTING THE MOST FROM THIS BOOK

Irresistible. Right from the start, let's define this word and how it will be used within the context of this book. When something is irresistible, it's alluring, magnetic, relentless in its persuasion. Something is irresistible when it can't be refused. The word connotes an incredibly strong draw. It's a banquet that you can't walk past without tasting its choicest fare.

The title of this book, at first glance, implies that a church can become irresistible to *people.* When certain initiatives are undertaken, a church becomes irresistibly inviting, and people can't help but be drawn to this church. I have no doubt that when the initiatives set forth in this book are followed, that sort of irresistibility will happen. When a church displays these qualities, the people will shout *Encore!* because they want it to continue and never end.

But becoming a church that's irresistible to people is not primarily what this book is about. That is actually the by-product of this book's premise. Here's the twist.

This is actually a book about becoming a church that is irresistible to *heaven.*

This book is about a church that heaven can't help but be deeply involved with, a church that God can't help but bless and use for His eternal purposes. It's a church that makes the angels shout *Encore!*

We are often apt to forget that the local church belongs to Jesus, not us. She is, or rather *we* are, His bride, and if we adorn ourselves for Him, His eyes will be on us for good. Forget this, and we begin to market ourselves for more members rather than posture ourselves for His manifest presence.

Success for a church may include marketing, facilities, and programs, but that is not what exclusively determines success. It is credited more to what I call the *Hand of God* factor. For more than thirty-six years (the time I've been in pastoral ministry), I've been an avid student of the Hand of God. Over the years, I've seen the Hand of God bless a church so that there is a favored season that lasts for decades. I've also witnessed other times when God's hand was on a ministry for the first several years and then lifted. I've observed this with church after church. During this process, I've collected principles to keep us postured for His grace and to rectify things when His hand seems to be lifting.

An irresistible church is not a perfect church. Rather it is one that is constantly aligning itself to pleasing God. It is a people who position their hearts carefully and deliberately with the tenets of the kingdom so that God is pleased to work in unrestricted ways. God is irresistibly drawn to a church where every activity, every plan, and every leadership decision clearly displays His heart.

This is a book about becoming a church
that is irresistible to *heaven.*

Among other verses, one biblical foundation for this premise is found in James 4:8. When we draw close to God, He draws close to us. In this passage, James pleads with us for commitment, cleansing, and contrition. These tenets, if followed, contribute to harmony and holiness within any local assembly. God's righteousness is extended and imputed to us because of the work of Christ on the cross, but we make the choice as to how close we draw to God. The closer we draw to Him, the more God is able to use us for His glory. In this sense, the closer our churches draw to God, the more irresistible they become to heaven.

And this church can be yours.

What does an irresistible church look like?

When you envision an irresistible church, a church that God loves to bless and can use in incredible ways, what comes to mind? Chances are it's a church that looks something like this:

- **You grow spiritually at this church.** An irresistible church fulfills its purposes. It is a local assembly that provides spiritual education grounded in biblical principles that help you and your family grow in faith. You trust this church's teaching. You can align yourself without mental reservation with the doctrinal stand of the church and commit yourself wholly to its position. It's also a place where you can worship God corporately with other people. It provides an opportunity to meet other Christ-followers and make lasting, authentic friendships.

- **You witness a strong sense of mission.** In the irresistible church, you see fruit: consistent conversions, lives being transformed, marriages healed, and new leaders being raised up.

- **You long to go to this church every week.** Simply put, you look forward to being part of its functions. If you miss a week, you're disappointed rather than relieved. You want to be involved because you know good things happen within and around an irresistible church.

- **You want to invest in this church for the long haul.** With an irresistible church, you feel no compulsion to "shop around" for a different church. There's a strong sense of satisfaction in connecting with the local assembly you're part of. You don't want to leave.

- **You tell others about this church.** You feel comfortable, even eager, talking about an irresistible church with other people—

Christians and non-Christians alike. You feel a sense of healthy pride in your church. You invite others to attend, and you're not worried about what will happen when they visit.

- **You relax at this church, knowing it's a model of growth, not perfection.** You don't expect or require flawlessness from an irresistible church. Mistakes are made, yet the people in your church own up to their mistakes, learn, and grow from them. An irresistible church is a model of grace and acceptance. People don't need to look or act a certain way to be part of the assembly. You bear with people, as people bear with you, and one of this church's unstated mottos is "We're all in this together."

- **You are delightfully challenged at this church.** You leave different than you arrived. An irresistible church educates, motivates, and empowers you each week with new tools for life. You are inspired to live differently because of what you have heard. And like the pair of travelers mentioned in Luke 24, you leave saying, "Were not our hearts burning within us while He was speaking to us?"

Any church can be irresistible

Do those bullet points describe your church? If so, that's a good thing. This book will help strengthen what you already know and help you develop and articulate the correct criteria for evaluating your church's effectiveness. Then you can help chart its course for the years to come.

But if the above bullet points are not reflective of your church, if they describe a church you only dream of and long to attend, then lean in closely: I've got a secret for you. Your church CAN become *irresistible*.

In the pages ahead, we'll look at twelve traits of churches with whom God is well pleased and subsequently people long to be a part of. People will always be drawn to places where God is actively involved with His people.

The story is told of a traveler who heard of the revival that was transforming Wales (1904–1906). People from far-flung countries began to converge on the town of Loughor. When his train came to a stop, the curious traveler asked a worker, "How do I find the church where Evan Roberts is preaching, the one where the revival is taking place?" The man replied, "You just start walking, sir, and God's presence will draw you in."

There's something irresistible about the genuine presence and activity of God. People don't need to see *us,* but they desperately need to see Jesus.

All the traits mentioned in this book are transferable. Use the study guide at the end of the book. Unpack these traits in your small groups. Discuss and process each question until you own it.

You have the power to help create the irresistible church you long to be a part of.

Remember, these qualities can be developed in *any* church. The exciting news is that *you* have the power to help create the irresistible church you long to be a part of. That's the secret we'll look at more closely throughout this book.

A church is so much more than a building. It is made up of individual lives, and collectively we comprise what the Bible calls the church—the bride of Christ. The more we grow to be like Christ, the more committed to His purposes we become, then the more involved in His mission we are. We have the power to create irresistible churches, because *we* are the church.

Perhaps you've just read the above lines with a bit of trepidation. You're thinking, *That may be all well and good. I'm glad I have the power to help my church go in a healthy direction. But I'm just one person. What can just one person do?*

It's a good question, one that can be answered two ways.

1. You have more influence in your church than you may think. Even if you don't have a formal leadership role at your church, you care deeply about what happens. You're a praying person, and prayer changes things. Or maybe you do have a formal leadership role in your church, but it's a comparatively small one. You're a small-group leader or you facilitate a Bible study group. Or perhaps your leadership role is larger. You're a pastor, elder, or board member. No matter your role, start where you're able. It's okay to start small. Take the principles outlined in this book and talk about them with the people within your sphere of influence, no matter the size of the sphere. You'll be surprised how the twelve traits catch fire among those with whom you interact.

2. We have both an individual and a corporate responsibility to develop the churches we're part of, and I encourage individuals to join together and study the principles in this book. Yes, it's healthy if an individual studies this book alone, followed up by taking steps to develop the traits within the local assembly. But imagine the possibilities for spiritual growth and renewal that could happen if a small group challenged itself to undertake the responsibility of becoming an irresistible church. Or further still, what might happen if an entire congregation worked through the principles outlined in this book, then committed to becoming an irresistible church together?

To that end, several helpful components are built into this book. Each of the twelve chapters focuses on one trait, and you can work through the material in one educational quarter at the pace of one chapter per week. At the end of the book, a study guide is available with questions for personal reflection or to use week-by-week as discussion starters for small groups. It also contains Scripture that will help you examine and apply the traits on a deeper level. This is a book designed with you in mind. Read it. Study it. Apply it. Then reap the rewards.

Getting from point A to point B

I've been in leadership meetings before, particularly in my earlier days of pastoral ministry, that I'd describe in hindsight as overly self-congratulatory. We were all eager to encourage one another. I guess that was because in those meetings we praised whatever activity took place; we equated activity with ministry. As a church, we were busy in Jesus' name, and we compared being *busy* with being *successful.* We praised what was average because nice people had headed up the activity and we didn't want to hurt anyone's feelings. We slapped ourselves on the back for working hard, for burning the candle at both ends, even though our pace was unsustainable and sometimes detrimental. In our drive to become influential in our communities, we were happy whenever we had good numbers at an event. But we weren't asking ourselves the more important questions about spiritual impact, whether lives were being changed and whether the presence of God was truly in our midst.

Developing the traits within a church does require honest self-evaluation—and that's not always easy.

The twelve traits outlined in this book offer a picture of what any church can become. The traits are realistic and attainable in their scope and practicality. But I must stress that developing the traits within a church does require honest self-evaluation—and that's not always easy.

Think of this book as a stand-up map near the entrance of a mall. A big red arrow on the map says *You are here.*

Where you want to go will inevitably be some distance from where you are now. This book will help you get from here to there. It will help you develop and articulate the criteria to honestly evaluate your church—not to criticize it, but to move down the corridors of the mall in the direction you long to go. Yes, the process requires honesty. And yes, the process requires asking the hard questions. I mention this up front simply to prepare you. Take courage. You can do it.

If a church does not have the traits outlined in this book, how does the church get from point A to point B? Is it simply a matter of the will? Or is it something more?

It's both.

Change must be empowered by the Holy Spirit, because true transformation is not man made. It's Spirit-led and Spirit-empowered. Yet we also must commit ourselves in such a way that the Holy Spirit is delighted to work through us. We must lean in the direction we're praying toward. As you read this book, read expectantly. Read prayerfully. Then get ready for good things. Get ready for action—because this book provides more than just good information.

Good information, if left alone, has an uncanny way of entering a person's head to simply provide knowledge, but if the information remains unused, it stagnates. Sometimes we don't actually want to make the effort to learn, we just want more knowledge so that people will consider us knowledgeable. But we must go beyond good intentions. This book aims to do more than simply inspire people. Inspiration is not wrong. People read a book and have an *Aha* moment, and it stirs their soul or warms their heart—and that's often needed. But I hope to get you beyond inspiration. There's a further step you need to take.

What I'm praying for is a *bias for action.*

An idea must enter a person's head in the form of knowledge, drop down to his heart as inspiration, then reach his feet, bleed out his toes, and get his legs moving! That's when lasting life change occurs. When a good idea gets shoe leather, a person transitions from being a Pharisee to being a disciple. He starts walking in the direction of that good idea, adding value to it. That's what I'm praying this book will accomplish.

> When an idea enters our head, it's called *information*.
> When it touches our heart, it's called *inspiration*.
> But when it bleeds out our toes and fingernails, it's called *incarnation*.

Please note that this book is *not* a blueprint intended to build each church so it looks precisely the same. I never want people to look at New Hope Oahu, where I'm the senior pastor, and try to impose on their church back home everything exactly as we do it. That creates inauthentic local assemblies as well as frustration.

Rather, I invite you and your church to discern the truths outlined in this book and then apply them to your own specific region and demographic. Create the irresistible church that fits you and the assignment God has given you. Adjust the traits outlined in this book so they become your church's values. Values are things that people (and organizations) put energy, attention, time, talents, money, and staffing toward. That's your invitation—to make it yours. You might even develop a healthy trait that's not outlined in this book. That's fine. The twelve traits produce an excellent list, one that's proven to work. But it's not exhaustive. Take the freedom to adjust the list to make it yours.

Create the irresistible church that fits you
and the assignment God has give you.

The DNA of change

We've talked a lot in this introduction about how change is needed—about how everyday churches can become irresistible churches by the process of transformation—and it's true, the word *change* has a way of scaring people off. People naturally resist change. It's seldom easy. Truthfully, the road to becoming an irresistible church does not happen without effort, even a bit of discomfort. But when we are truly walking with Christ, He invites us to healthy change. It is part of the transformational process we need to make a regular part of our experience.

The Japanese have a unique word for a lifestyle of change: *kaizen.* And it means "change that heads toward constant improvement." Excellence is not something we achieve once and then cruise on forever after. Excellence requires constant development. More *kaizen* is needed in our churches. It's where change for the good becomes a consistent part of who we are. We adapt. We grow. We reach new people in new ways. Second Corinthians 3:18 describes how we "are being transformed into his likeness with ever-increasing glory." That transformation is part of the *kaizen* process. The church must yield herself to God, allowing Him to constantly move her toward God's best.

A life well stewarded

I invite you to read this book with confidence. It has been distilled from over thirty years of studying, honing, and applying these traits. We've planted more than one hundred ten churches in our three decades of existence, so you can quickly surmise that our mistakes far outnumber our trophies and accolades! We've seen our share of challenging times. But that's just the point. There's an Old English proverb that says, "A smooth sea never made a skilled mariner." Our church has sailed through some stormy seas in the past and survived those rough waters. To use another metaphor, the chaff has been blown into the wind, and this book contains the lasting wheat kernels of what we've learned along the way.

And here's the grace part: We've seen over 83,000 people make first-time decisions to follow Christ during the past two decades!

I need to be crystal clear about another point up front: Becoming an irresistible church is not about becoming a big church numerically. I'm not trying to get you to become a big church. Blessing is not always about numbers. At its core, blessing is about spiritual impact. I've seen small churches become irresistible churches and have tremendously powerful spiritual impact. I've seen big churches do nothing but increase numbers and have a lot of hype and activity. And I've seen everything in between.

Blessing is not always about numbers.
At its core, blessing is about spiritual impact.

Let me reiterate the core of the book. The traits examined in this book are not primarily what are required to become an irresistible church to visitors. That will be a result. The true bottom-line invitation of this book is to *become an irresistible church to heaven*. That means we become a church that heaven can't help but get involved with and bring increased ministry to. You'll find many ideas to optimize how we treat people and increase attendance, but the irreducible principle is intentionally posturing our hearts and positioning ourselves to be in His grace.

The bottom line to flourishing under God's hand of blessing is faithfulness. It is about knowing God's will and then doing it. It doesn't matter the size, the age, the location, the denomination, or the history of your church. Every church is invited to be faithful to God's will. Every church can run in the pathways of His command, for He has set our hearts free (Psalm 119:32).

That's good news for you and me. Because, let's face it, there has never been a greater need than now for more churches to do what they need to do. We have about 370, 000 churches in this nation, and we collectively spend about seventy-five billion dollars annually on church-oriented products, yet the spiritual impact on our cities is often negligible. This past season in the state of Hawaii alone, we needed to send two thousand inmates back into the community because we didn't have enough room in our jails. People blamed the lack of tax dollars, the pervasiveness of drugs, and the breakdown of the family. But I say blame the church, at least in part. We're not doing our job of impacting society as it needs to be done.

There is hope. Irresistible churches can be cultivated. Irresistible churches are champions at leading people closer to God, being conduits for the Holy Spirit to change lives for the better and impact society for good. When we find out who we are, and are fully settled on doing what God has asked us to do and be, then we don't have to move far to find Christ and live for Him. Our days aren't wasted doing the wrong things. Our lives are well stewarded.

That's the promise of this book. The point of an irresistible church is never to simply see its members attend church each week and then do nothing. It's to attend, be equipped, and then go out and live purposeful lives for God. A church must be a place where disciples gather—and then *scatter*. St. Augustine said, "A man's chief end is to glorify God and to enjoy Him forever." The invitation held out in these pages is to make our lives matter for what counts. Living a life well stewarded is our responsibility and our opportunity. We can create irresistible churches, churches that help change the world. The solution starts with us, because *we* are the church.

Irresistible churches are champions at leading people closer to God, being conduits for the Holy Spirit to change lives for the better and impact society for good.

If that sounds like something you'd like to be involved in, I invite you to keep reading.

AN IRRESISTIBLE CHURCH HUNGERS FOR THE PRESENCE OF GOD

Some years ago, we were notified that the high school auditorium we normally use to hold our services at New Hope Oahu would not be available for one weekend in February. The school we rent from is very gracious, and we had received notices like this before, but they usually came six to eight months in advance. Profuse with apologies, school administrators handed us the memo. This time, we needed to vacate in *six weeks*.

The gargantuan task of finding another spot for our weekend services suddenly stared us down. We began knocking on doors. We tried our local Aloha Stadium, public halls, the university, any place large enough to hold ten thousand people. But nothing was available; nothing . . . except our last option—an outdoor park. The problem was our Hawaiian weather. It is unpredictable and often uncooperative during the spring months. One day it's blue skies; the next it's pelting rain. We had no other choice, so we reserved the park and initiated an emergency prayer program to persuade God to keep the skies blue . . . at least for one weekend.

As the time approached, we made our preparations. We rented a larger-than-life sound system, hundreds of lights, and copious amounts of staging equipment. Our plan was to hold three services instead of our regular five—one Saturday evening and two on Sunday morning. The tent to protect the stage looked like a gigantic airplane hangar. Another tent, sufficient to hold about one thousand, was erected so a few people could find shelter if the rains came down. There were no other tents available to rent, so everyone else in attendance would need to sit under, hopefully, the canopy of stars for the evening service and blue skies for the morning services.

As the weekend approached, the weather did not look promising. When our first service began Saturday at 6:00 p.m., a light drizzle misted down, but we remained steady. The service concluded with most of us damp but agreeable. Before retiring that evening, I thought it wise to meet with the Chief Weatherman and log my concerns. My respectful plea began, "Lord, you know how I've served you faithfully for lo these many years. I have not asked of Thee long life nor for the life of mine enemies." (When I get serious, I tend to use the 1611 language of the King James era.) "I beseech Thee for sunshine on this Thy beloved people who shall gather in the morn that we might praise Thee . . . un-wetted."

Satisfied with my supplication and mastery of biblical language, I drifted off to sleep. The following morning, however, I was awakened by the sounds of pelting rain. Quickly I got back on my knees, and this time, I spoke plainly: "Dear God. We can't have this! Turn off the faucet . . . puleeze!"

Mustering up all the confidence I could, I walked toward my car without my umbrella, believing with devoted assurance that by the time I reached the park, the rain would stop. As I drove down the street, raindrops attacked my windshield. Unfettered, I refused to activate the windshield wipers, in faith, believing that it would be clear skies ahead. All that did was make it hard to see the road! By the time I arrived at the park, the worship portion of the service had already begun. Like a saturated sponge, a huddled handful of faithful followers were singing in the rain. I joined them. Our postures might have been identical, but I will bet that the content of our hearts was not. With outstretched hands, I raised up not hymns, but protests of complaint: "God!" I objected, "may I remind you again just how long I have been serving you? I ask for one favor . . . just one insignificant favor! And what do I get? I can't believe this."

"You are more concerned with the absence of rain than you are about the presence of God."

I remember His voice. It wasn't an angry voice, but it was firm. I don't know if anyone else heard it; but for me, it parted the heavens. "You are more concerned with the absence of rain than you are about the presence of God."

That's all I heard. Everything stopped, or at least it seemed that way. The music stilled. Time ground to a halt. God was right. Without His presence, a sun-filled sky would only make it that—a sunny day. But with His presence, even a rainy morning could be the beginning of a revival that would transform the islands.

The little message that I believed was from God echoed within me. I knew I had been more interested in the absence of problems than I was in the presence of God. I remember crying out for His presence, and in light of that perspective, my concern about the rain paled in comparison. We continued the service, I with a renewed heart for His manifest presence. By the end of our time together, the skies had parted and the most beautiful sunshine bathed His people with a clearly understood affirmation of His attendance.

More of Him

The first trait of an irresistible church, a church God loves to bless, is a hunger for the presence of God. That might sound strange initially, considering Scripture's teaching on the omnipresence of God. God is Spirit; He has no physical form. He is already present everywhere in the universe, and everything is in His presence. Matthew 18:20, for instance, says, "For where two or three come together in my name, there am I with them." God declares in Jeremiah 23:24, "Do not I fill heaven and earth?" Nothing is hidden from Him, and nothing escapes God's notice.

Yet when we talk about hungering for the presence of God, its definition includes at least three vital components. First, it is a greater realization of God's presence. God is already present, yet we want to perceive His presence more. We want to be more conscious of Him. We want a greater awareness of Him in our midst. God promises that as we draw near to Him, He will draw near to us (James 4:8), and Scripture indicates that we will experience His presence in ever-increasing measures as we hunger for Him.

Second, when we hunger for the presence of God, we long to be filled to full measure with His Holy Spirit. Although the Holy Spirit's presence in a believer is a constant, Ephesians 5:18–20 indicates that our experience can vary by the degree of His power and presence operating in our lives. We are filled with the Holy Spirit when God occupies every part of our lives. He is allowed to do within us all that He came to do. He guides and controls us. His power is exerted through us and reveals itself in the fruits of the Spirit: love, joy, peace, patience, kindness. (See Galatians 5:22–23.)

Third, when we talk about hungering for the presence of God, we may include the request for a special anointing for a special task at a specific time. We call this God's manifest presence. It is a clear, even visible increase of God's working in a specific situation, event, or life. For instance, a special outpouring of God's power may flow through a meeting, or touch the lives of people in a marked way, or be evident in a particular way for a specific season of revival. Psalm 145:18 offers a glimpse into this presence: "The Lord is near to all who call on him, to all who call on him in truth."

An irresistible church longs for God's presence more than anything.

As a caveat, we need to be careful whenever we discuss the manifest presence of God, because people can sometimes misuse or even abuse this privilege and seek overly emotional, erroneous, even dangerous or fanatical spiritual experiences. Simply put, any experience that happens under the umbrella of seeking the manifest presence of God always needs to be in alignment with God's revealed will in Scripture. God's manifest presence will always honor the person of Jesus Christ and produce a greater hatred of sin and a greater love for righteousness. It will never contradict any previously revealed truth found in the Bible.

Taking all three components into consideration, seeking the presence of God is of utmost importance in our churches. One man quipped, "You could take the Holy Spirit out of half the churches in America and they would keep right on going as if nothing happened." This reality is abhorrent, especially in these last days. An irresistible church longs for God's presence more than anything—more than spacious facilities, cutting-edge programs, large attendance, big budgets, or rain-free days.

Abraham Lincoln's prayer

I like to remember the core of what it means to seek the presence of God with this story: Abraham Lincoln was not only a great president, he was a man of God. Most faith-based speakers before ascending to the podium are likely to pray, "Without you, Lord, I will fail." But Abraham Lincoln prayed, "Without you, Lord . . . I *must* fail."[1]

Do you see the difference? President Lincoln's prayer was a dangerous prayer. It was also deeply honest and courageous and powerful. He knew that people—by their sheer willpower—are capable of harnessing great human resources to carry out great activities. He knew that people could drum up impressive programs, undertake important initiatives, and maintain positive momentums.

Yet he wanted something greater than anything human made, something undeniably of divine origin and implementation. President Lincoln did not want to succeed unless God was at the root of his initiatives. If God was not at the center of his mission, he did not want his mission even to exist, much less thrive.

Churches, by nature of being spiritual climates,
are often unwilling to acknowledge
a lack of God's presence.

May President Lincoln's prayer—*Without you, Lord . . . [we] must fail*—be the prayer of our churches as well.

If God's presence is not sensed in a church, what can be done? Let me suggest three actions a church can undertake to change this direction.

1. **Recognize the vacuum.** This is an important first action, because churches, by nature of being spiritual climates, are often unwilling to acknowledge a lack of God's presence. A church, however, will seldom take action to move toward something better unless it first realizes the need. Take a short mental survey of your church's current atmosphere. To what degree do any of the following symptoms of vacuum apply?

Fruitless. In this situation, a church is characterized by a lack of love, joy, peace, patience, kindness, goodness, gentleness, or self-control. Likewise, little spiritual impact is taking place. It's been a long time since the church has seen a person come to Christ or seen a baptism.

Wordless. People aren't reading the Bible, the Word of God. Little emphasis is placed on the Word in each week's message. People aren't living out biblical practices or basing their lives on the principles and laws found in God's Word.

Careless. Spiritual disciplines within a church have become more about routine than relationship. Little excitement for spiritual matters is in evidence.

Visionless. People seem more interested in the logistics of running the church than in the church's spiritual impact. Discussion about the color of the carpet and similar such matters supersedes concern about where souls will spend eternity.

Missionless. There is more interest in getting people in the doors of the church than equipping people for service in order to send them out.

Numberless. A faulty emphasis is placed on counting nickels and noses rather than salvations and baptisms. Or a church fails to see the overall bigger picture of lives changed. (Some of the impact of this, ironically, can never fully be counted.)

Purposeless. People worry about how the church looks to others rather than how obedient the church is to Christ. The church values performance and image above heart, faithfulness, and obedience. The church uses different measuring tapes than God uses.

2. **Fill the vacuum with what is righteous.** The second action to take when seeking the presence of God is for individuals within a church to sync their hearts with heaven. It's a simple

concept: Think of syncing a heart to heaven the same way a calendar is synced with a laptop. When they're in sync, they're in agreement. With this leaning, we regularly plug our hearts into heaven's heart so that we see what God sees. We value what God values. Whatever touches God's heart touches our heart. We pray, work, and lean toward reversing everything on the above vacuum list.

John Wesley's words have hung in my heart for seasons. He said, "I value all things only by the price they shall gain in eternity."[2] What does heaven value aside from the Word of God and people? For example, we might not think a particular strained relationship may count for much here. But it matters a lot in heaven. Or a small treasure might be worth a great deal here, but little in heaven. When we fill the vacuum with what is righteous, we value all things only by the price they shall gain in eternity.

3. **Purposely exhibit tangible, visible signs of faith.** This might sound like a strange action to take when seeking the presence of God, but I have found it to be very helpful. Certainly tangible, visible signs of faith begin in the heart, and we always need to address heart issues as of utmost importance. Yet faith will often follow action when action is visible first. Therefore, I recommend that churches decorate their church environments with the landscape of the values of heaven. That is, use the physical bricks and mortar in any way you can to further the message. For example, when we want to move in the direction of God's presence, it's helpful to keep a church's mission statement where everybody can see it—on walls, on letterheads, on Web sites. Keep the true functions of a church in places where everybody can be reminded of them. Hebrews 2:1 says we must pay closer attention to what we have heard lest we drift away. Our natural tendency is to drift from mission. We're not inclined to become more strategic in mission.

The human heart always drifts into entropy, selfishness, or worldliness. So we've got to paint our atmosphere with the colors of heaven to help align our hearts with heaven and with one another.

When all of heaven is silenced

How do we recognize the presence of God in our midst? Certainly the experience will always be in line with Scripture, yet I do not know how God will specifically choose to show up in your assembly when you long for a greater sense of Him. I do know, however, that something God-honoring takes place whenever we hunger for Him.

Once, for instance, I was asked to speak at a small country church. It held maybe eighty people, and before the message, three young men, perhaps nineteen to twenty-one years old, led us in a time of worship. The congregation sang mostly hymns: "Amazing Grace" and "Just a Closer Walk With Thee," and they sang loudly, with great gusto. Yet no matter how loudly we sang, I could hear these three young men over everyone else. Heart, they had, but singers, they were not. I must confess that I wanted to put my fingers in my ears—it was the type of off-key singing that can make your insides cringe. I started talking to God about it, complaining, actually, hoping the young men would soon release me from the pain. Just then the Lord, with a gracious but reprimanding tone, said: "I have silenced all of heaven in order to hear them and witness their hunger for my presence. I suggest you do the same."

Something God-honoring takes place whenever we hunger for Him.

I am reticent to be overly dramatic, so I hesitate to share about another experience, but there have been many weekends at New Hope

Oahu where we've prayed for the presence of God, and an actual visible mist has emerged and lingered inside the auditorium as God's Word was spoken.

It's a strange phenomenon, one I can't fully explain. The first time I noticed it I had to blink to be sure it was not my contact lenses fogging over. It has repeated itself several times—and no, I don't equate it with some sort of natural phenomenon whereby Hawaii's ocean air combines with warm bodies in a sanctuary. The mist is different than a person would experience in a bathroom after a steamy shower, or rising from a warm roadway after a thunderstorm. I know without a doubt that God's presence is in this mist.

I've never written or spoken publicly about it, and honestly, I don't put that much stock in it lest people get crazy about seeking the mist instead of seeking God. We don't emphasize experiencing outward manifestations of God's glory. It's always about the gospel, about seeing changed hearts and lives because of the work Christ has done on the cross. So whenever I have seen the mist, I have not called attention to it. I have simply continued on with the message from the Bible and enjoyed a warmer sense of God's gentle presence. Quietly, I remind myself of Zephaniah's words: "The Lord your God is in your midst. . . . He will exult over you with joy, He will be quiet in His love" (Zephaniah 3:17 NASB).

Speaking of weather and God's presence, in twenty-six years of baptizing people in Hawaii, including eleven years in Hilo, the rainiest city in the state, it has almost always rained the day we have scheduled baptisms. Since the beginning of New Hope Oahu, we have baptized more than 16,000 people at our local Ala Moana beach, and baptizing people outside when it's raining tends to create logistic problems—not for the people getting baptized, they're going to be wet anyway—for the people in attendance.

Yet each time we have gathered at the ocean's shores during a rainstorm, the Lord has parted the clouds and allowed the sun to shine. Once when we were praying for the baptism candidates, we were huddled under umbrellas in the pouring rain. I mean *pouring*. We prayed. And as soon as our short trek to the water began, the showers halted and a circle of sunshine spotlighted the event as if heaven were revealing to us a hint of God's delight. It seemed that a hole opened up in the sky right around where the baptisms were taking place. Sunshine radiated through in a perfect cylinder. It was as if God was saying, "You're doing good—this is what I'm asking you to do." When the last baptism was done and we moved to get lunch, it started to rain again.

He is God.
How He chooses to make himself evident
is up to Him.

Your church will undoubtedly experience God's presence in different ways than ours. I'm not advocating that your church seek poorly trained yet heartfelt worship leaders or an auditorium filled with mist, or even an outdoor baptism where God parts the storm. I'm advocating your church doing business with God. I'm advocating all of us turning from the sins that so easily entangle us, and running with perseverance the race marked out for us (Hebrews 12:1–2). Let us all fix our eyes on Jesus, and love Him, serve Him, and enjoy His presence more and more. He is God. How He chooses to make himself evident is up to Him. Amen.

ACTION STEP: Seek the presence of God.

AN IRRESISTIBLE CHURCH REMEMBERS WHO SHE IS

The picture on the coffee canister caught him cold. The man blinked, rubbed his eyes, and peered over his grocery cart at the image on the Taster's Choice coffee canister sitting on the store shelf. The face peering back at him was unmistakable. The sideburns were darker, and the lines around the eyes weren't there yet, but it was clearly him—Russell Christoff—an unassuming fifty-eight-year-old kindergarten teacher from Northern California. Christoff picked up the coffee can and showed it to a clerk. "Yep, that's you all right," she said. "Wow, you're famous."

Christoff bought the can, and then headed to a lawyer's office. A legal dispute began with the coffee company. It seems sixteen years earlier, Christoff had been working as a part-time model and had posed for the picture along with several other models who tried out for the role. Company representatives told Christoff that if his picture was ever used, they'd call him back and finalize the contract. No call came, years went by, and all was forgotten. Then one day an employee pulled the photo to use in an advertisement, evidently believing consent had been given. The picture was printed. And printed, and printed, and printed. For six years it showed up on coffee canisters sold all over the United States, Canada, Mexico, Japan, South Korea, Israel, and Kuwait.

When the dust settled, a jury concluded that Christoff's picture had indeed helped the company sell coffee. Lots of coffee. And it had all been done without Christoff's permission. The court awarded Christoff a payment that included more than 5 percent of the company's profits from Taster's Choice sales for the years the photo circulated. His award: 15.3 million dollars!

What's the moral of the story?

It pays to know who you are!

Here comes the church

Whether you are a pastor or layleader, you must never forget who you are. Israel kept forgetting what their main assignment was on the earth, and they went down rabbit trails. Let's think about our true identity for a moment—both as individual believers and as a local assembly, for this is the second trait of an irresistible church, a church God loves to bless: We know who we are. If we follow Christ, then we're part of the body of believers that comprises the universal church. Our true identity is a glorious one. It's an identity that positions us for action. Our invitation is always to remember our true identity, and then to act on that identity.

I realize that's not always easy to do. Part of the difficulty with remembering and acting on our identity is that the word *church* is used to describe more than one thing.

A church can mean a building or a group of people who gather together for worship. It's used as a synonym for congregants or churchgoers, or sometimes for the leadership or decision makers within the local assembly. We say that "the church decided to call a new pastor" or that "the church down the street is doing an outreach event tonight."

The word *church* is also used for a service or meeting in which we do things that we've come to understand as church. So we say, "Are you going to church today?"

It can refer to a denomination, a group of congregations centered on certain beliefs, practices, and projects, such as the United Methodist Church.

Further still, the church—sometimes with a capital *C*—is used to describe all believers in Christ. It's the church universal, or all people who profess to know Christ as Savior and live for Him. When we say that the church is the bride of Christ, we mean it in this sense.

This book talks about at least three uses of the word, at times almost interchangeably, and it does so for a reason. The church is us. We comprise the universal body of believers. And the church is also a local gathering of the universal church. We are the church (His people) that meets at the church (building).

On one hand, when we talk about the title of this book, *The Irresistible Church*, it means a local assembly that people can't get enough of. Yet, of much more importance, it means that we've remembered our true identity as the bride of Christ and are living in light of that identity. The title means we're in the process of developing the traits that make us glorious as a bride. Ultimately, a church is irresistible because a church reflects Christ's glory—and Christ is the One who's truly irresistible. People really don't need to see us. They need to come in contact with Him each weekend.

And remember: Your church will be no more involved than you are involved. She will be no more devoted than you are. No more genuine than you are. No more positive than you are. Why?

Because you are the church!

The bride, the soldier, the family

Let's examine a church's true identity more closely. Can you picture a bride on her wedding day? She's resplendent in glory. Her gown is exquisite. Her hair is perfectly done. You can see her confident smile from beneath her veil as she walks down the aisle. Altogether, she's a vision of beauty, brilliance, hope, and promise. This is her special day, the day she's dreamed of her whole life, and as she takes her place at the front of the sanctuary next to the groom, she knows she's deeply cherished and highly valued. And the groom can't resist her.

That's the picture of the church and Christ. Christ loves us as intensely as a groom loves his bride. The metaphor is found in at least two places in Scripture—Revelation 21:9–10, where the church is called the wife of the Lamb, and in Ephesians 5:21–30, where the apostle Paul exhorts husbands to love their wives "just as Christ loved the church."

Our identity is a glorious one indeed, and remembering this true identity is the second trait of an irresistible church. When we remember who we are, we're able to act on who we are. We're able to fulfill our destiny and live purposeful, satisfied lives where we don't waste time on the wrong things. You and I only have one run on this earth. If we mess up this one, we don't come back again for a do-over. Each day we live right now is an integral part of the one life we've been given. When it's all over, we want to be able to stand before God and hear Him say, "Well done."

As a caveat, I want to acknowledge that some people, particularly men, have a hard time with the concept that we're a bride. The image is too feminine, too other-worldly. If that's you, don't worry—the Bible provides several other metaphors that describe the church's true identity. Second Timothy 2:3–4 describes us as soldiers of Christ. That image is often easier for men to grasp. Visualize Christ as your company commander. He's your guide. He's your captain. He's the man out in front who takes us through the battle. Under Christ's leadership, we're an elite group of volunteer soldiers, similar to today's Green Berets or Army Rangers. It's a privilege to be led by Christ, the epitome of courage, honor, and valor. Again, the point is that when we remember who we are, we're able to act on who we are.

First Peter 2:9 describes the church as "a chosen race, a royal priesthood, a holy nation, a people belonging to God." The idea is similar: The church is called out, chosen, valued. Picture the church as a royal family—esteemed and set apart for service. God's love for us is strong, and Christ is eternally committed to the church, His people.

The church is loved and chosen,
empowered by God, and set apart for service.

It doesn't matter which biblical metaphor we use to remember our identity and then act on it. The metaphors all point to the same thing—the church is loved and chosen, empowered by God, and set apart for service. The bride metaphor is used mostly in this book simply because it feels like the most glorious one to me, and the big idea of this book is that when the church lives in light of its true identity, then it becomes irresistible. But if it helps to think of the church's identity as an elite soldier or royal family, that's fine, too. The point is that our identity is an attractive, empowered, purposeful one. A bride is so captivating that people can't help but be drawn to her. They want to stand in line to greet her after the ceremony. They want to dance with her at the reception. That's the idea I want to get across—that the church can be as winsome as that bride.

We can find great joy and satisfaction in our true identity. Like Russell Christoff, we are rich beyond measure—even if we don't yet realize it. Our riches don't come from earthly possessions, from cars, houses, or fancy jewelry. Rather, the book of Colossians says that our riches are found in the heavenly realms. Christ saved us. He forgave us. He chooses us to do important service on earth. We have a hope and an eternal future with Him in glory. The work that Jesus Christ did for us on the cross has provided all we need to be accepted by an infinitely majestic, powerful, and holy God.

Christ invites us to live in this richness. We're not beggars or bandits. Christ offers abundance. Second Peter 1:3 indicates that "His divine power has given us everything we need for life and godliness." This means we have all the power needed for spiritual vitality. We can victoriously live in light of Christ's ministry. We are able to worship God wholeheartedly. We do not need to be enslaved to sin. We are able to care for people and accomplish humanitarian and social justice efforts. We are able to love others as Christ loves us. We are able to be and do as Christ invites us to be and do.

That's the church's true identity. We are the attractive bride of Christ. We're strong, capable, and confident because Christ loves and empowers us.

So what's the problem?

A church has a tendency to forget.

A case of mistaken identity

A friend of mine told me a story about something that happened during his college years. His final exam required the completion of a certain book report that would yield 50 percent of his grade. He worked long and hard on this assignment, completed it, and turned it in. Several days later, he received the book report back. Scrawled on the front cover in bold red ink were these words: "Great content. Excellent bibliography. Outstanding research . . . Grade: F. Wrong assignment!"

When he told me his story, it took me two days to stop laughing. For weeks I would chuckle whenever it came to mind.

But there's a sobering parallel to the story. I wonder if God will say something similar to numerous churches one day: "Nice-looking church building. Wonderful greeters. Highly relevant music. Well-organized small groups . . . Grade: F. Wrong assignment!"

A wrong assignment is when a church forgets her true identity. What might that look like?

- **A forgotten identity is when a church becomes busy doing the wrong things.** When a church is busy, it often believes it's doing the right thing. A church can be filled with activity. Meetings are held. Songs are sung. The church secretary's master calendar is filled to the margins. But if all that activity doesn't lead to spiritual transformation, a church is focused on the wrong initiatives. All that busyness is like a man roofing a building using cardboard. He hammers away until he's sweaty and breathless, but when the rain comes, the roof turns to mush.

A church's emphasis should never be more on "come here" than on "let's go out there."

- **A forgotten identity is when a church becomes an end rather than a means to an end.** A church's emphasis should never be more on "come here" than on "let's go out there." If we function under the belief that our only task is to get people into a church building, then we're spending time working on the wrong term paper. The true end of a church is to influence society so that people come to Christ and lives are transformed. A church I know so wanted to remember its true identity that it hung a sign over its front door on the inside of the church building. As people headed outside they read: "You are now entering the mission field." That's what our true identity is all about!

- **A forgotten identity is when the Christian subculture sets in or becomes too prominent a focus in a church.** Are you familiar with the Christian subculture? It's when we have our own fashions, our own music, our own theater, films, books, and conferences. The Christian subculture is generally characterized as safe and nice, so it's easy to gravitate toward it and settle in. Many of the products geared solely toward Christians are not wrong in themselves. They genuinely serve a purpose by educating or ministering to Christians. But God never intended that we be a subculture unto ourselves. Rather, He asks that we be a counterculture, a culture that does what's true and right and good even when darkness is all around it. He asks that we remain in the culture, that we be *in* the world and yet not *of* the world, so that we can be influencers in "a crooked and depraved generation, in which [we] shine like stars in the universe" (Philippians 2:14–15).

The light within space

The good news is that we can remember our true identity and then act on that identity. It's true that the term *church* can be used of a gathering point, a building, a place where people meet each week for instruction, fellowship, worship, and equipping. And that definition is correct. I'm not asking that we forget that purpose of a church. Hebrews 10:23–25 indicates that one of the functions of a church is to be a place where disciples regularly gather. This is a good function of a local church, to be a stopping place where people meet each week for good purposes.

The church must always be a means
to something far greater.

But if that's the only identity we have, then we've missed the point. When a church forgets her identity, when she becomes busy doing the wrong things, or she becomes an end in herself, or she becomes too focused on the Christian subculture, then the pioneer spirit is quenched, and the bride of Christ is always supposed to be a pioneer bride. That's a curious mixing of metaphors, but the Lord says we're sojourners, citizens of heaven. We're here in temporary form only. We must never lose the heart of a pioneer bride, a heart that's always adapting, changing, seeking to live out our true purpose and reach a dying world for Christ. Once a pioneer becomes a settler, then the means becomes the end, and that's the beginning of the real end. The church must always be a means to something far greater.

I like to think of the church's role in society this way: Imagine looking up at the sky at night—what do you see? Aside from the moon and stars, the rest of the sky looks dark. To us, space looks black. But astronomers tell us there is actually a great deal of light in space. The reason space looks so dark is that there are no reflective surfaces that catch and show the light. If some sort of solid matter such as a planet is introduced, then the light is seen.

The church is like that reflective matter. The Bible calls us a mirror of Christ, the countenance of Christ, the representation of Christ (Matthew 5:14–16; 2 Corinthians 3:18). He is the light, and we are the reflection of that light in a darkened world. Our invitation as believers is to go out into the darkness of the world and reflect the light of Christ. The point is not that the world see us, it's that the world see Christ. That's what a church is called to do.

And that's irresistible.

ACTION STEP: Remember the true identity of the church, then act on that identity.

AN IRRESISTIBLE
CHURCH LIVES
HEART FIRST

A beautiful nine-year-old girl, Lin Miaoke, appeared in the opening ceremonies of the 2008 Olympics in Beijing. She belted out "Ode to the Motherland" to the applause of the world. Yet the world has since discovered that she was not singing. She was only performing.

The song had been recorded by seven-year-old Yang Peiyi, whose appearance didn't make the final cut. Yang Peiyi was still getting her front teeth in, so they were not perfect. Most seven-year-olds would be able to relate, but Chinese officials pulled her from the stage because a Communist party official decided her looks were not suitable.

The spokesman for the Olympic organizing committee, Sun Weide, explained: "We decided to let Lin Miaoke sing on stage and to use Yang Peiyi's voice because Yang Peiyi has the best voice, while Lin Miaoke is the best actress."[1]

That was a nice spin; but when you think about it, best actress is actually a thin euphemism for best image. Of course, we surely do not blame either of the young girls, but it does perpetuate the myth that a Hollywood-esque image is everything. The illusion is that if we look good, then we must be good.

Right?

Wrong!

Where's the heart?

The third trait of an irresistible church, a church God loves to bless, is living heart first. It's the opposite of living image first. It means working and serving God with true passion. It means living with an intrinsic desire to travel the pathways down which God invites us.

I am not suggesting that competency within a church isn't important. Heart and excellence are not mutually exclusive. In other words, it is not either/or. It is both/and. A common tendency is to use heart as an excuse for being sloppy. But when we live heart first, excellence usually follows. An irresistible church may have some crooked teeth and not everyone may sing in perfect pitch, but that doesn't keep people away. It's when the image wears away and they see that we've been lip-syncing that everything loses its luster.

When we live heart first, excellence usually follows.

That's what happened to us. In the pioneer days of New Hope Oahu, all we had was heart. We couldn't afford image. We didn't have proper chairs; we sat around cafeteria tables in a makeshift arrangement. We didn't have instruments; every musician used his own. We set up a gauntlet of greeters, eight on each side; and when people arrived, they were funneled between our grandstands of huggers. We would later be coined *the hugging church,* known for converging on anyone within ten feet. We sang with all our hearts. We served with all our hearts. We set up and took down with all our hearts, and the church grew and grew. I remember praying in the early days of New

Hope: "God, please, let us one day have our own chairs, our own sound system, and maybe even some paid staff with our own office." I didn't mind working out of my briefcase at a coffee shop, but it wasn't long before our discipleship groups filled the dining area. The coffee shop manager kindly asked us to find a larger venue, shrink our influence, or buy out his coffee shop. As the months passed, we saved enough money to rent our own office space. We bought our own chairs and purchased our own musical instruments. We had our own sound system and even bought our own vans. We felt we had arrived.

One day, however, a woman's innocent comment returned me to what was most important. She remarked, "We have such talented musicians and such wonderful services at this church. Yet I remember the early days when we had little or nothing. I am sure it's still there, but it's hard to see anymore. Where's the heart gone?"

She was right. Our church had flat-lined. We had begun new programs and new initiatives and we were carrying on with our existing ones, but when we were honest with ourselves, we saw that the completion of tasks and the maintenance of our week-to-week operations had become more important than anything else. Although the heart of New Hope was still present, it was no longer emphasized.

That night I spent some extra time in prayer asking for God's counsel. I honestly cannot tell you that this was an audible voice, but I knew it was His instruction nevertheless. Paraphrasing, I heard Him say, "Correct back to the heart. Peel away whatever you need to until the servants' hearts are once again visible. In the end, a mind will reach a mind, but only a heart will reach a heart." God directed us to reemphasize the importance of our hearts. And so we did. A heart focus is what God used to spiritually grow our church then, and it is what God would use to spiritually grow our church in the future.

Over the next season, we pruned any program or task that relied more on image than heart. We culled initiatives that were based more on talent than on character. No sacred cows were safe.

We emphasized both individual and corporate responsibility in drawing near to God. We knew that when our hearts were close to His, the church would follow.

A mind will reach a mind,
but only a heart will reach a heart.

We restructured until we could see the light of genuine hearts again. Since then we have worked to continually live heart first.

I do not want to suggest that programs or maintaining programs is the enemy of the church. In years past *program* has almost become a dirty word in some church circles. But programs are only organized forms of ministry. They are not wrong. They are needed. They can be useful tools. The important distinction for us to make is that a program does not always equal ministry. Just because a program is in place, it does not necessarily mean that lives are being impacted for Christ.

The danger comes when our programs outgrow our hearts. Usually in the beginning of any ministry-oriented initiative, we lead with our passion. We take more risks. We develop things with a sort of raw energy. Yet once a program is implemented, the temptation exists to slip into autopilot. We rest, thinking the program will continue to endlessly produce the same results. The problem is that our hearts start to depend on the programs. We can have programs going, but no heart behind them.

For instance, just because we've got small groups up and running in our church does not mean that true community is taking place within our church. Or just because we have an altar call every Sunday does not mean true evangelism is taking place. Or just because we have men's ministry at our church does not necessarily mean that we are producing better husbands, fathers, brothers, friends, and community leaders.

Specifically, I advocate regular examination and reevaluation of every program within a church. I encourage churches to fearlessly dig to the core and find out why a church does what it does. Do not be afraid to kill ineffectual programs that have lost their purpose. Do not be afraid to do fewer things in a church, if it means being able to do fewer things well. Certainly, the principles of effective leadership apply in times such as these. A church often operates like a big ship. You don't turn on a dime when steering an ocean liner and it's often wise to kill ineffectual programs slowly and patiently, making small, purposeful changes in structure, staffing, locations, or emphasis.

But we must always get to the heart of it, and stay at the heart.

If your life depended on it

Much of the path to creating irresistible churches begins with us. We are the church, and whatever enriches us enriches the greater body of Christ. If I'm walking closely with Christ, then it's going to show. If I love my place of service within the church, no matter how large or small that place is, then my place of service is going to sparkle and radiate. Whenever we serve out of willingness rather than drudgery (1 Peter 5:2), we serve out of an overflow, not out of a vacuum. The first is natural. The latter feels contrived. If we work on ourselves harder than we work on the church, then the church becomes an automatic beneficiary.

If you are not in a position of church leadership, you may be asking what you can do to help your church return to its heart. You may not be able to spearhead the creation, design, and implementation of effective church ministries, yet I encourage you to undertake the process of living heart first within your own life. *You* follow Christ. *You* live with passion and calling. Throw your heart into your sphere of influence.

Does this take effort? Absolutely. And anytime something requires exertion, people are prone to step out the side door early. I include myself in this common temptation. Yet I wonder what would happen if we began to really live like our lives depended on it. Think about that phrase for a minute—*living like our lives depended on it*. Do you know what I mean by it? It's when we purposely live with a full degree of passion. We throw ourselves into what matters.

To illustrate, from time to time in my position at the college, I have students approach me who say things like, "I can't get a good grade in this class. I don't know what to do."

If I sense it's a matter of making time for priorities, I'll ask, "Well, what if your life depended on getting an A—what would you do then? Imagine you need an operation that costs $200,000 but you don't have insurance and can't afford the surgery. If you don't get the operation, you will die. So you come to me for help and I say to you, 'I'll pay $200,000 for your surgery, if you get an A in this class.' Do you think you'd get an A in the class?"

"Absolutely," the student says.

Why the change? It's because the student is now living like his life depended on it.

What would happen if all of us chose this approach to life? How would it affect our schooling, our work, our relationships, our churches? We can change the world if our hearts are fully engaged. But for the most part, we don't live this way. We think programs are going to do the job for us. Or we take the easy road. We see this all the time in our churches. People set themselves on cruise control and nothing further happens. We might long for effectual life change, but we're waiting for a new speaker, or a more dynamic worship team, or a better-flavored coffee in the lobby, or some sort of miraculous writing on the wall to produce the results for us.

We can change the world
if our hearts are fully engaged.

To live like our lives depended on it does not mean we burn out for Christ. It literally took heart surgery for me to learn that lesson. I used to run nonstop from early morning until late at night before my body forced me to slow down. I still run hard, but now I've learned to strategically place several rest stops along the way, places where I can slow myself down and consciously be grateful. These rest stops along life's highway allow me to live more deeply. I only make commitments after I am convinced that this is what Jesus is asking of me.

Living like our lives depended on it means living with sustainable excellence. When we choose to live this way, then we're serving with all our hearts, we're worshiping with all our hearts, we're feeding ourselves spiritually with daily Bible reading, prayer, intentional fellowship, and acts of service. When we live heart first, we become irresistible as a church.

I stress again that living heart first does not come accidentally. It is produced and then maintained only by vigilant monitoring. The human tendency always drifts toward selfishness and ease, and only through a conscious daily effort will we break free from the ruts.

But it can be done. In fact, you can spot people who live heart first. They exhibit three important characteristics. We all have the ability to live this way, thanks to our will and the power of the Holy Spirit at work within us.

The three characteristics of living heart first are:

1. **Being quick to forgive.** People who live heart first overlook flaws and crooked teeth. They mentally and emotionally extend forgiveness to people who wrong them, even though that person may never actually come and ask for forgiveness.[2] People who live heart first live with the freedom that comes from not holding a grudge. There's a lightness to their step, a spiritual buoyancy that comes from not carrying extra baggage. They are quicker to pray the line from the Lord's Prayer, "Forgive our debts, as we forgive our debtors."

2. **Having a larger capacity to receive godly correction.** People who live heart first welcome improvement even though it may be delivered by unconventional means—a child, a boss, a mother or father, an in-law, a critic. The correction and resulting improvement usually happen in small ways, again and again. Years ago I took golf lessons; the instructor must have pointed out at least ten times a certain thing I was doing with my swing. The error was ingrained, a muscle memory I needed to break, and it took those ten reminders before I was finally able to correct it. In a similar manner, instruction through the vehicle of correction can become a tool the Holy Spirit uses to free us from deeply ingrained habits. It's like driving down the freeway. Even though the road looks straight, we can't simply tie a string from the steering wheel to the radio knob and go to sleep. We need to make repeated slight corrections in order to remain in our lane. People who live heart first recognize this and receive correction with humility.

3. **Living a surrendered life.** People who live heart first willingly yield their plans to God's plans. They don't set aside their desires, per se, because they remember Psalm 37:4, where God promises to give us the desires of our hearts. Yet they live with Proverbs 16:9 in mind: "In his heart a man plans his course, but the Lord determines his steps." Mother Teresa, one of my heroes, taught me much about the surrendered heart. Before she died in 1997, she directed the Missionaries of Charity, where she ministered for over forty-five years. A Nobel Peace Prize recipient, she worked with those who had contracted HIV/AIDS, leprosy, and tuberculosis. Her Catholic order ran soup kitchens, children and family counseling programs, orphanages, and schools. She surrendered to God's plans and lived out her famous words "In this life we cannot do great things. We can only do small things with great love."

Giving God room

The title of this book—*The Irresistible Church*—means being irresistible to the presence of God. Our invitation is to become churches that are irresistible to heaven. That's what we want our churches to be. The key is to yield our plans to God. We need to make sure our hearts are postured to give credence to divine intervention.

Several years ago, an elderly friend of mine needed knee surgery. It was scheduled, but the day of the surgery, he was sent back home. Why? A few days earlier, he had caught a cold. The doctor told him that in order for the surgery to be successful, he had to be well. I couldn't understand the reasoning at first. After all, the surgery was to be on his knee, not his nose! But what the wise physician knew was that the energy required to heal after knee surgery would be depleted by his body's immune system trying to fight his cold. He needed to be positioned to heal, postured to recuperate.

People who live heart first
willingly yield their plans to God's plans.

It's not always easy to do. We have preconceived notions of what God wants in order to do His miraculous work. For some, it may be thrilling worship. For others, it may be the presence of spiritual gifts or charismatic preachers. But it may be the complete opposite in an irresistible church.

Some years ago New Hope Oahu held a talent night. We gathered our brightest and best on stage for an evening of concert and drama rich in ambience. From the opening presentation, the full house of enthusiasts knew this would be an evening to remember. Brilliant dances, extraordinary solos, enchanting dramas, and beautiful choreography graced the stage. I sat spellbound, realizing how endowed with talent we were as a church.

Then toward the end of the evening, the lights dimmed and one of our special children appeared on stage. Nikki has Down's syndrome. She and her parents began attending the church when we first started meeting years earlier in a school cafeteria. She appeared confident and convinced that she was supposed to be there, but I must confess my first reaction was apprehension.

Certainly I worried about what would come next. Sadly, my concern wasn't for Nikki's sake as much as for our church's reputation. Yes, I feared our being judged by the visitors. Yes, I was afraid of what people would say. One of the greatest fears of man is being seen as a failure in the eyes of others. But God was tearing that away. God was looking at the heart.

A few awkward seconds passed. Then Darlene Zschech's worship song "Lord, I Give You My Heart" spilled over the sound system. Using American Sign Language, Nikki began. Her hand motions and demeanor looked increasingly confident with each passing lyric, reminding us of the One who gave His life. I felt myself relaxing, being drawn to the truth of this reminder. As I surrendered to the Holy Spirit working through this moment, I felt something deep down in my soul being recalibrated.

The Lord reminded me that a church can push for professionalism or a church can make a case for being folksy, and neither is correct if we make the mistake of thinking both or either are routes to godliness. The key is giving room to the Holy Spirit. It means we always give God the veto rights to whatever happens in our churches.

That's what God did that evening when Nikki signed the worship song on stage. It was like God pulled me aside and said, "Wayne, how does that grab you?" My choice was either to humble myself and see the heart, or harden my heart and remain proud.

The anthem concluded. With hands upraised, Nikki stood as if empty—held together only by God's pleasure. All activity in heaven seemed stilled for the moment. Overcome with emotion, tears and audible sobs overpowered our good manners, and we broke into a standing ovation with shouts of "Encore!" That evening found us gathered together before the throne to remind us of what God delights in most.

ACTION STEP: Choose to live like your life depended on it.

AN IRRESISTIBLE CHURCH PRACTICES GRATEFULNESS

Sometimes God sends us a divine directive to be still so He can restore us once again. He intentionally removes the hurry from our steps in order that we might correct our cadence.

It happened to me a few years ago when I received an unexpected invitation from God. After several months of chest pains, I was diagnosed with three blockages in my heart. I was put on the next plane to Stanford Medical Center in California. Four days later, after a successful surgery, my blood count was still low, and I found myself tiring easily. So instead of hurrying back to work, I took a detour to our family farm in Oregon. There our two daughters, son-in-law, and two grandchildren live happily alongside thirteen chickens, three dogs, four cats, and one cow. God was inviting me to experience a new form of success. He was inviting me to slow down and be grateful for what I had.

Early one morning shortly into the visit, I drove to a nearby coffee shop for my devotions. It was autumn, and I found myself noticing the countryside as I drove along the back roads. Usually I'm in too much of a hurry to notice the beauty of God's creation, but that morning I purposely responded to God's invitation and slowed my tempo. A fog lay like soft cotton on the meadow, shrouding it gently. Circling the surrounding hills, a wispy haze created the appearance of a passing train that left in its wake a disappearing trail of steam. Then, like a slow-rising curtain, the receding fog revealed a choir of verdant cedars, reminding me of Psalm 98:8, "Let the mountains sing together for joy." That morning played out like the opening act of a divine musical that displayed God's splendor. All around me, creation trumpeted the majesty of God.

I found myself grateful and renewed in the moment. I also found myself learning a valuable lesson in sustainability from the Lord. Simply put, I needed more moments like that. I needed to regularly and purposefully slow myself down so I could notice God's handiwork and express more gratitude. An old rabbinic saying I heard years ago came to mind: "God will one day hold us each accountable for all the things He created for us to enjoy, but we refused to do so."[1] For too long, my refusal had come in the form of my hurriedness. By not stopping at life's scenic lookouts, I had not been enjoying the landscape as God intended. Too much of the time, I was in too much of a hurry to get on with business.

A person who lives an irresistible life must ruthlessly remove all hurry, for life happens "in between." Using a musical metaphor, Noah benShea, the insightful writer, penned these perceptive words: "It's the space between the notes that make the music."

Have you ever noticed how God can slow us down on purpose? The slowing might seem random, even annoying at first, but if we look closely we can see God's good and perfect hand at work. God slows us down for a reason. He invites us to be still, to see the circumstances around us as evidence of His sovereignty. When we are still, we are invited to become more grateful. Gratefulness takes our eyes off what's wrong and focuses our hearts on everything good and pure and true and right and admirable (Philippians 4:8). If we are mindful not to wrestle against God's process, we can see that the slowing actually leads to God's best for us, even though it might not seem so at the time.

Knowing how to be still—does that characterize your life and church?

When a prayer is answered no

The fourth trait of an irresistible church, a church God loves to bless, is gratefulness. I believe God is more concerned about our being grateful than just about anything else. A spirit of gratefulness is developed whenever we pause to notice a rainbow or refuse to rush past a sunset. When we take the time to notice, we feel arising in us a deep appreciation that wasn't there before. We are again reminded that we are surrounded by things we don't deserve but have been granted nonetheless.

I believe God is more concerned about our being grateful than just about anything else.

God's artistry is not limited to the beauty of a rural countryside. It is evident everywhere—yes, even in churches—if only we will stop to notice. Gratefulness is discovered when we remove the hurry from our lives and listen to God's voice in a situation. A situation may seem imperfect, but being grateful anyway is evidence of our trust in Him.

Gratefulness differs from thankfulness. Both are essential. Thankfulness is the cordial response to a favor done. It is the affirmation we give when things go our way. It is the reply to a gift or a promotion; it's the hooray after a blessing.

Gratefulness, however, is different. It can only be developed intentionally. It begins with a spirit. It's an attitude, a disposition that we carry and practice whether or not things go our way. Gratefulness means being content before any gifts are given—or even if they're not. It's breathing a silent thank-you regardless of our circumstances. Gratefulness is a hallelujah even when there's no guarantee of a blessing. It is the confidence to accept whatever God brings.

In 1995, my wife, Anna, and I moved from Hilo, Hawaii, to Oahu to start a new church—New Hope Oahu. We had already been pastoring the New Hope Hilo church for twelve years and planted nine others, but we sensed God calling us to plant a church that would serve Oahu and beyond.

The new church was an exciting work, and as the church in Oahu began to flourish, we wondered if the Lord was leading us to construct a church building. We began to pray. In the meantime, we rented a location at a high school. It seemed like it took so much work each week for teams of people to set up and take down everything we needed for our services. Undoubtedly, we told ourselves, it would make better use of the Lord's resources if we had a permanent location. But month after month, year after year, the answer seemed to be no.

The reason we couldn't acquire land to build was simple. One acre of Hawaiian real estate sells for about 2.5 million dollars. We needed a minimum of twenty acres; so doing a little math, we could see that meant we needed fifty million dollars just for starters. Even if we could afford those prices, finding twenty contiguous acres available anywhere near Honolulu was basically impossible. Still, we felt we could trust God for a miracle. We knew that He owns the cattle on a thousand hills, and he owns the hills as well. Making a church building available to us would be no problem to Him. We prayed, and kept on praying. But still, the answer was the same. In that season of waiting, we could have been impatient. We could have grumbled. We could have focused on what was *wrong* with the situation.

Or we could have chosen to be grateful.

Fortunately, we chose the latter. We realized that we could either complain about what we didn't have or we could be grateful for what we did have.

Ironically, more than fifteen years later, we still don't have our own church building—and we've realized that we probably never will. But we've also realized that it's all worked out for the best. We have become one family in many locations, linked together by a common heart for Christ, a love for one another, and a video feed.

We longed for a building because it seemed the thing to have. But we chose to be grateful because we knew the Lord was in control. Now, even though we still don't have a church building, we've become a stronger network of churches. The situation has allowed us to invest the money we would have used on a building for other kingdom-building purposes. And the situation has proven beneficial, personally, to me as a pastor. I've learned to play less and coach more, and that's been much healthier for me—as well as for the church. Today we have a lead pastor over each campus, and I oversee the lead pastors. My job is to encourage them, applaud, cheer, and inspire. They're doing a fantastic job. The system that God led us to develop allows me to hold an additional position as chancellor of Eugene Bible College, where I'm investing in leaders again. It's a result that only God could see all those years ago, and it has allowed me to be more effective, not less.

Sometimes, God holds His cards close to His chest. God knows the chemistry and the wiring of each one of us. A season of slowness, of not getting exactly what we pray for, of having something that's less than perfect, makes us depend on Him more. It makes us be more grateful for each day. It invites us to be thankful for what we have. It prompts us not to rush ahead, because even though we don't know what the future holds, we know God holds the future. Allowing God to be in control is much better. A season of slowness keeps us close to Him who holds the cards. That's what God wants. He doesn't want us to just look at the cards and run with the hand, He wants us to stay close to Him.

That's one of the biggest—and most difficult—lessons a church can ever learn. If something seems lacking in your church, even when you pray for it, and continually pray, and keep praying—and God's answer still seems to be no, then trust Him through the process. Trust Him anyway that His answer is best. Be grateful that God is leading your church in a good path, even when you don't see the outcome. God sees the outcome, and God is always good.

Be grateful that God is leading your church in a good path, even when you don't see the outcome.

Our choice of colors

I firmly believe that gratefulness is our decision. We have the power to choose whether or not to be grateful. In Matthew 6:22–23, Jesus said, "The eye is the lamp of the body. If your eyes are good, your whole body will be full of light. But if your eyes are bad, your whole body will be full of darkness."

Jesus is referring to how we perceive life. One person paints things darkly while another person paints things brightly. Our choice of gratefulness defines the colors on our palette. One person's tray holds only grays while another's bounces with neon colors. We choose how we will paint situations, setbacks, and circumstances.

What colors will you choose?

Gratefulness searches for colors of splendor. It takes the time to see the grandeur within the simple. It keeps in mind the big picture of a church—that we're all family—and sees all people within that family as valuable contributors. When we choose to be grateful, we can respect the wisdom that's etched into every line of an elder's countenance. When we choose to be grateful, we can look past the pierced lip and tattoos of an edgy twenty-something young person and see great potential. Every stroke of the brush must be intentional if we are to paint a masterpiece.

One specialty brush we can use to help us be grateful is true evaluation. Typically, we evaluate according to our likes or dislikes—our preferences—because that's what we're used to. As such, we evaluate our churches much the same way we would evaluate a movie or a theater performance. As we walk out the door, we give whatever we've just seen a thumbs-up or a thumbs-down, depending on whether or not we liked it.

But true evaluation uses a different paradigm—one that evaluates according to purpose. Using this paradigm, we don't necessarily need to enjoy something to consider it a success. Rather, we ask ourselves if something has accomplished what it was supposed to do. True evaluation will factor in the criteria of intentionality. Something is successful (or not) depending on the fulfillment of its design or its faithfulness to a calling.

As a church leader, for instance, I might poke my head around the door of a youth meeting from time to time to see what's going on. What kind of evaluation will I use—preference-oriented or purpose-oriented? At my age, I might not personally enjoy the type of music that's being played, or I might not want to participate in any of the kids' zany icebreakers. Yet if I correctly evaluate the ministry based on its purpose, then I can see that the type of music and icebreakers are reaching the intended audience—teenagers. As such, I can correctly evaluate a program or ministry. My evaluation is not based on my *preferences*. It's based on *purpose*.

When we know about this type of evaluation—and practice it—we see our churches less as commodities (places we attend and receive goods and services) and more as communities: local spiritual assemblies built around people journeying to become more like Christ. Practicing true evaluation is a tremendous tool in helping us become more grateful. We are freed from liking or not liking our churches, and can appreciate them based on their design and faithfulness.

Seeing the possibilities

If gratefulness is not a regular trait in our church experience, what can we do? One of the best practical ways to learn gratefulness is simply to begin to show gratefulness. When we begin with the action, then our hearts will follow. It's as simple as finding someone doing something right and telling him so. This practice puts us on the high road to fruitfulness.

Our call is never to be false in our expressions of gratitude. I'm not advocating finding someone doing nothing and flattering him with false praise. But I do advocate the lessening of our expectations of flawlessness, particularly within a church. A church family is a mix of people, all with differing talents, gifts, interests, and opinions. When we sincerely practice gratefulness, we factor in the diversity of our mix. When we are consciously grateful, for instance, we are reminded that sometimes a speaker has an off Sunday, and that's okay. Or we acknowledge that sometimes a friend misunderstands us, even as we sometimes misunderstand him. We recognize that some of the songs in a worship set don't resonate with us. Our gratefulness reminds us that we are all sinners saved by grace, and only God is perfect. Our practice of this trait allows us beautiful breathing room in our relationships and interactions.

Gratefulness hears the sounds of what could be, even what should be, and it guides us with hope. Gratefulness causes us to focus on God, who is perfect in glory. It is the gateway through which our days may dance. Gratefulness reminds us of all the gifts that we should not have been given, the friends we do not deserve, and the grace we did not earn.

Gratefulness reminds us of all the gifts that
we should not have been given, the friends we do
not deserve, and the grace we did not earn.

It is easy to lose this fragile gift. Gratefulness is readily displaced or unwittingly exchanged for want. It slumps into entitlement and tricks us into thinking that we deserve more than we do. Instead, gratefulness is to be cherished and carefully maintained. It is to be exercised in the shadows as well as in the footlights; equally in the extravagant as in the common.

One of the habits Anna and I have is to periodically remind each other to be grateful. I recall when we bought our first home, a 780-square-foot house. It wasn't much, but we would often comment to one another after returning from a long day, "What a beautiful home we have!" Of course, it wouldn't attract any interest from *Better Homes and Gardens*, but we were grateful nevertheless. It was more about the condition of our hearts than the condition of our house.

Each weekend, I drive onto the high school campus where New Hope has held weekend services for over a decade, and I consciously practice gratefulness. I notice the many tents that have been set up the night before. I see our parking attendants who have arrived at 5:00 a.m. and other volunteers who have helped transform the school's seventy-year-old auditorium, once slated for demolition, into a palace fit for the King. Tears blur my eyes and I am once again reminded of the treasure we have in our midst. As the Sunday services continue, I remind myself of the myriad people who are giving their time to teach Sunday school, serve coffee, hand out bulletins, and minister through our worship teams. I infuse each week's experience with gratefulness, and reminders of gratitude are consciously and continually on my lips in prayer.

No matter the circumstances, you can find things about your church to be grateful for. Some of you reading this book will be in churches that were built on the deep commitments of men and women who have gone before you. It may be humble but beautiful, small but just right. It's never the size of the building that makes a church irresistible to heaven. It's the size of heart that's in the building that makes it irresistible.

It's a lesson I'm continually learning—how to consciously slow myself down and see the beauty of God's creation. I was reminded of this recently through the words of a volunteer. All our receptionists at New Hope are volunteers. It's been that way since our inception. One dear woman has been doing this every Wednesday for more than five years. A while ago, I approached the front desk and stopped to acknowledge her faithfulness and thank her for taking her only day off to answer phones and greet visitors.

"Oh no!" she replied. "I look forward to this all week long. This is where my soul finds rest and my heart is uplifted! I should thank you."

Now, that's a church I long to be part of, one where gratefulness is seen on an everyday basis. It's a trait that echoes back to the glory of God. It's part of what can make a church irresistible.

ACTION STEP: Consciously and regularly practice gratefulness.

AN IRRESISTIBLE CHURCH PROMOTES HEALTHY RELATIONSHIPS

Some years ago, I conducted a leadership seminar in a midwestern town. Following the sessions, I stayed an extra day to meet with a local board whose church was navigating a pastoral transition. While preparing for my meeting, I was in a restaurant eating breakfast. Suddenly a man in his early thirties slid into the booth directly across from me. "You're Wayne Cordeiro!"

"Last time I checked," I said with a slight smile.

"I'm a new pastor. Our church has flat-lined. I need some resources. You have a new book? A new tape? Maybe some fresh ideas for leaders like me?"

Now I laughed audibly. "Hold on," I said. "What's happening?"

"Our church needs help. We're stuck. We've tried dozens of new programs and spent thousands on conferences. But there isn't any program, no matter how much I hype it, that seems to work. They all die!"

He had my attention, so I pressed him further. "How long have you been the pastor?"

"Nine months," he replied.

"That's not a long time, but enough time to give birth," I quipped. "How did you come to pastor this church, anyway?"

He began the story slowly, choosing his words more carefully. "It wasn't good," he said, shaking his head. "The conflict happened on a Sunday morning. Our last pastor walked up to the pulpit. I thought he was about to begin his message, but instead he said, 'Could I have the elders stand?' One by one, the seven elders stood. The pastor then said, 'It's because of these men that I'm leaving this church.' Then he picked up his Bible and promptly walked out."

"No way!"

"Yup. I was the assistant pastor at the time. That's how I became the pastor."

I let out a nervous laugh, "The conflict didn't happen on that Sunday."

"Oh, yes it did. I was there!"

"You may have been, but it didn't happen that Sunday." Now he was confused. I continued. "The conflict may have come to a head that Sunday, but it happened months—maybe years—before, when leadership began to tolerate broken relationships within the congregation. The seething anger of unresolved problems was stuffed underground, and people accepted it as normal to live incongruently. No, the conflict may have come to the surface that morning, but it had been festering for a long time."

The other pastor nodded. He recounted several incidents where the wheels first began to slide.

He and I talked further for some time. We were able to narrow down the problems and identify possible solutions to help mend relationships within the congregation. Later, back in my car, I was saddened to think that I had heard many similar stories of church conflict. Perhaps none as dramatic as the pastor who called into account his elder board during a Sunday service, but plenty of stories abound about unresolved and ongoing disputes in churches.

When a church has healthy relationships, people are genuinely excited to see each other. That ongoing sense of exuberance is observable to veteran attendees as well as visitors. But when unresolved problems are tolerated, the resulting unsettledness wreaks havoc on a local assembly like weeds on a plowed field. Visitors detect the inevitability of a bad crop even though they might not be able to pinpoint where its specific origins lie.

Resolving conflict is of paramount importance in a church, although it is seldom easy. But it can be done—and done on an ongoing basis—in your church as well as in mine.

A normally tidy house

The fifth trait of an irresistible church, a church God loves to bless, is having healthy relationships. It's when people get along with each other. It's when a church promotes and encourages a sense of unity in the bond of love. Possessing this trait doesn't mean everyone in a church always agrees with everyone else or that there are never any problems. It simply means that when problems do occur we take the time and effort to resolve them in a timely manner.

Ironically, it can be refreshing, even freeing, to acknowledge the inevitability of problems within a church. No church is problem-free, nor should we expect it to be. When we realize that problems commonly creep up in any local assembly, we are released from the pressure of needing to have everything look tidy all the time.

Think of it this way: My wife keeps a clean house. That doesn't mean our house never gets dirty, particularly with our three children and the grandkids around! But it means that when our house does get dirty, it doesn't stay that way for very long before it's cleaned up. Every healthy church that's growing has one thing in common: problems. The same is true with families and marriages. Problems are often signs that people are trying their best. For example, when people dance their feet often get tangled. But they don't quit there. They simply untangle and keep dancing.

People are sometimes tempted to push problems under the rug, hoping that if a conflict is ignored it will work itself out in time. Certainly tact and diplomacy need to be factored into any dispute, and sometimes that means encouraging people to overlook an insult (Proverbs 12:16) or certain wrongs (1 Corinthians 13:5). Yet in most disputes, particularly if they are serious in nature or involve larger groups of people, some sort of overt conflict resolution will be required. The DNA of any conflict resolution involves bringing people together and getting them to talk to and listen to each other. Specific interests will need to be sorted out; rumors will need to be overturned or clarified; common goals and areas of understanding will need to be searched for and found; and apologies will need to be made and accepted. Each step along the way takes time, effort, patience, and prayer.

God is faithful to bring healing when it is sought, and we can have a hand in deciding how long it will take if we yield to His principles. One radical plan involves canceling Sunday services until everyone in a church has given each other a clean slate. I know it sounds pretty radical, but I am not the one making this outlandish request. Jesus did. In Matthew 5:23–24, He gives this startling instruction:

> Therefore, if you are offering your gift at the altar and there remember that your brother has something against you, leave your gift there in front of the altar. First go and be reconciled to your brother; then come and offer your gift.

In other words, Jesus is saying that having right relationships with one another is more important than having church. These words of Jesus are strong words. They are a command, not an option, even though certainly we are to discern to what degree this command needs to be applied. For example, it may be overreacting to cancel services until a dispute between two individuals within a church is resolved. Yet in a dispute that is systemic, involving all or most of a congregation, I would suggest that this dramatic response of canceling services is highly appropriate.

Jesus is saying that having right relationships with one another is more important than having church.

Regardless of how this passage is applied to each situation, the overarching principle holds true: Relationships between individuals are of utmost importance. Churches are living organisms; they are not corporate organizations. They are active entities made up of living people—and people need to get along with each other. The health of an individual affects the health of the whole church.

If an individual is fundamentally happy and healthy, barring any catastrophic accident, he will seldom get sick. If he does, he won't stay sick very long. On the other hand, if that same person is under a weight of unresolved problems, anxieties, buried fears, and unsettled hurts, his immune system will be severely affected. He will become vulnerable to sickness and will soon surrender to illness. And when he does get sick, he will stay sick for a long time.

Churches are the same. When a culture of healthy relationships is compromised, we are at risk of a variety of diseases. We become predisposed to unnecessary relational illnesses. These include a lack of communication, a diminishing joy, and an increase of gossip. When relationships are thriving, our spiritual immune system protects us from random illnesses. If we get ill, we are resilient and we heal quickly. This results in a tangible joy, camaraderie, and mutual support as people work together as a team.

When Brad Pitt brings pizza

I do not mean for this chapter to be primarily on conflict reso-lution. There are other good resources church leadership can use to walk congregants through conflict on an in-depth level. Sometimes a church will need to hire outside consultants to help lead a body through intentional conflict resolution, particularly if the church has a history of disputes, or if it is transitioning between pastors when the parting has not been mutually agreeable. The process usually involves sorting out power struggles, clarification of roles, confession, restoration, and healing. Calling in consultants or intentional interim leadership is almost always time well spent.

Rather, my intention is to point us to the positive side of this trait—that an irresistible church fosters healthy relationships. What's the single best way of doing this? Having a common goal. At our church, we put our nine core values in writing. We put these values all over our walls. We take specific time during weekend messages to teach our core values to people. And it works. We always want to keep the big picture in mind of why we exist as a church.

When I think of individuals coming together to work for a com-mon goal, I like to think of celebrity fund-raising events. Have you ever seen these on TV? They usually take place after a catastrophe occurs. Celebrities come together and rally around a cause, all work-ing together for the common good. George Clooney mops the floor. Whoopi Goldberg answers the phone. Brad Pitt brings in pizza. Our skeptical sides may wonder at the public-relations value in the celeb-rities' altruism. Yet I want to suspend skepticism for a moment and examine the overall healthy model of setting aside individual interests for the sake of a greater good. At one recent event, a reporter asked, "How do you get all these multimillion-dollar celebrities to help out like this?" And someone said, "Because something much bigger than us is happening right now."

That phrase contains much value. The church needs to operate much the same way. The Holy Spirit loves to work in an environment of genuine affection, where people know that the larger goal is not about them; it's about the Messiah being born, it's about Christ coming into the world, it's about eternity invading our lives. That's where the excitement is. When we see each other and work together as co-laborers, comrades, partners, allies, we're acknowledging that we're all part of the redemption plan of God.

When a church rallies around a common goal, it helps foster a culture of people wanting to be together. In a society that resists closeness, healthy relationships offer a cure to loneliness. Genesis 2:18 reminds us "The Lord God said, 'It is not good for the man to be alone.' " We were created in such a way that apart from one another, we cannot be fulfilled. Mother Teresa once said: "If we have no peace, it is because we have forgotten that we belong to each other."[1] We can never forget that.

One of my dearest friends is a man named Noel Campbell. He is in his golden years now, but for several years, he was a mentor to me as I cut my teeth as a young upstart pastor. At that time, POG collecting was the rage. These desirables were wax bottle caps with the moniker of a dairy imprinted on them. Aficionados of these collectibles predicted that POGs would surely outvalue baseball cards one day.

Anticipating my newfound wealth, I traded, bartered, and haggled with the best of them. Satisfied with my stash, I approached Noel one day and asked: "Noel, I'm about to get rich. So let me ask you . . . some collect baseball cards while others collect POGs. What are you collecting?" Noel's reply took me by surprise.

"I collect friends."

Programs, facilities, resources, and organizational charts only begin to make sense in the context of healthy relationships.

Have you ever heard another person say something perceptive and thought, *I wish I had said that*? My friend's comment was long before the days of Facebook, where one might aim to collect friends as sheer numbers on her page. Noel said it sincerely. He loved people and desired to spend much time in the propagation and cultivation of fellowship.

For a church, it is paramount to operate from the principle that programs, facilities, resources, and organizational charts only begin to make sense in the context of healthy relationships. Healthy relationships set the stage for lifelong friendships. Under these conditions, friendships coalesce. The rest is secondary.

The smell of freshly baked apple pie

Throughout my travels, I have encountered irresistible churches in every shape and size, churches where individuals continually work past their differences and enjoy healthy fellowship. These churches can be found in prominent settings as well as in obscure ones. An important part of being an irresistible church is that people simply enjoy being with one another. It's when churches collect friends and truly mean it.

Sometimes, when this trait of healthy relationships is overtly evident in a church, there is no need for impressive programs or expensive venues. I remember one Sunday night in the middle of the winter. I was in a small church hall where the congregants were celebrating the seventy-fifth birthday of one of their members. As the people arrived, they greeted one another as if it were their first encounter after a long winter's hibernation. The old woodstove wasn't able to keep pace with the size of the room, so most just kept their jackets buttoned. The walls were faded. The floors were cracked. The setting was humble, yet people's genuine affection for one another made everything seem lavish. No one took notice of the surroundings. Instead, laughter erupted around the room as people traded memories and we dined on freshly baked apple pie. The unfettered candor in that church was absolutely refreshing. The people didn't have much, but good hearts combined with a good God made those present feel as if they were the most special people on earth.

Where healthy relationships exist, the Holy Spirit will be delighted to attend. He will be thrilled to fill the humblest surroundings with the presence of God.

ACTION STEP: Keep the greater goal in mind.

AN IRRESISTIBLE CHURCH IS ALWAYS LEARNING

A specific group of Bedouin sheepherders called the Tatars regularly traversed the landscape of Siberia around the sixteenth century. In order to survive, they followed the food supply of grass and available vegetation for their herds. They had to be ready to strike camp as soon as their food source could no longer sustain their flocks, and they were ever on the hunt for desert water holes and fresh pastures. The Tatars were characterized as a docile people, mostly quiet and unassuming. On rare occasions, however, when they would get angry, a certain phrase they tossed to their opponent or antagonist summed it all up. Through pressed lips and red faces, these stern words were heard: "May you stay in one place the rest of your life!"[1] The phrase seems tame at first glance, but when we picture the survival imperative placed on the Tatars' herds and families, we understand the severe nature of this curse.

As churches, we tend to lean the other direction: We favor stability over change. Often our greatest unspoken goal is to arrive at a good place and stay put. We like the programs we're already familiar with. If something worked last year, or the year before, or even ten years before that, we are tempted to use it again. One of the unspoken values of many churches is consistency, and consistency is often equated with *keeping things the way they've always been.*

But an irresistible church chooses to constantly learn and adapt. The church recognizes change as the currency of a constantly shifting society, and what worked yesterday to minister to that society may not always work today. An irresistible church does not change for change's sake alone. The main emphasis is never placed on being relevant, current, or "cool." Rather, we must choose to change because God uses the agent of change for His good. God knows that once people stop learning new things, they stop growing. The human spirit thrives on learning about God, His will, others, and even itself.

Futurist Alvin Toffler wrote that "the illiterate of the twenty-first century will not be those who cannot read and write, but those who cannot learn, unlearn, and relearn."[2] That is our task as a church as well. In order to continue ministering to a changing society, we must continually adapt and change. Likewise, in order to be the people God wants us to be, we must continue to learn, unlearn, and relearn.

An important factor in learning

The sixth trait of an irresistible church, a church God loves to bless, is the ability to constantly keep learning. One of the best vehicles for helping us learn comes from an unlikely source: the mistake. Few people, me included, enjoy making mistakes. But if we take time to purposely reflect upon our mistakes, much wisdom can result.

Several months ago during a question-and-answer session at a seminar I was giving, a young man in the audience raised his hand. "How often have you made major mistakes in your life?" he asked.

"On the average, about once every week since birth," I said.

There was immediate laughter, but I interrupted with, "The question for all of us, however, is not whether or not we've made mistakes. The real question is what have we done with those mistakes?"

If we take time to purposely reflect upon our mistakes, much wisdom can result.

This is the climate of constant learning we aim to foster at New Hope Oahu. It's okay to try new things, to take risks in ministry, to be courageous in effort and originality. Even though we've been established and functioning as a church for a number of years, New Hope Oahu is still a church of mostly young leaders in the early stages of discovery. When we began, we could have hired only veterans, but very early, our senior leaders chose instead to be coaches, coaxing out potential from novices.

We have learned along the way that emerging leaders are a joy to work with. They keep us on our toes and our knees at the same time. In retrospect, I am glad that we decided to develop young leaders rather than hire only veterans. I would do it all again, but there has come one great realization: Inside every young leader are hundreds of mistakes just waiting to be made. Of course we are neither casual about errors nor are we cavalier about misjudgments. But we need to make adequate room in all our churches for young leaders to find their way back if they have the fortitude to improve. Martin Luther once said, "Love God and sin boldly!"[3] He wasn't encouraging us to sin intentionally. Rather, he meant that in our effort to love God, we will be prone to making mistakes, and if we are afraid of making mistakes, we may not be able to serve God fully.

It's helpful to adopt the attitude of King Solomon as we think about our church environments. Solomon said it with wry wit: "Where no oxen are, the manger is clean, but much revenue comes by the strength of the ox" (Proverbs 14:4 NASB). It was Solomon's way of saying that if our goal is a clean manger, we won't have any strength or effectiveness. But if we want strength and effectiveness, we'd better buy a shovel. Errors in judgment, faults, and blunders are not fatal, for the most part. But what can be deadly is the way we deal with our failures. How we respond to them will often determine the degree of damage that occurs. So here is what I do: I squeeze out every last drop of wisdom that mistakes will allow me. I learn whatever I can, and then I throw the empty carcass of that mistake over my shoulder and never think of it again. Mistakes deserve a quick funeral and a slow reflection. Which brings us to the next important component of the trait of always learning—reflection.

The examined life

Making a mistake enables us to have experience, but experience alone makes us none the wiser. When we repeat a mistake, experience only reminds us that we've done this before. It is not experience, but reflection that brings the desired wisdom. The equation I use is this: Experience plus reflection equals insight.

Are you one to reflect on your life, including the mistakes you've made? I do not endorse spending copious amounts of time rehashing mistakes. Rather, I simply advocate leading examined lives. Do you know what I mean by that term—an *examined* life? Some people's lives are like blank notebooks. They never write anything in them. No notations. No reflections. No experiences. Other people's lives are like notebooks filled with experiences, but once recorded they are never visited again. Their notebooks simply contain the records of past failures. Others, however, regularly invest time to reflect on their experiences. They invest in seasons of solitude, both short and long, in order to consider what God is teaching. It takes time and reflection to correct wrong perspectives and redefine life priorities. These avid students of insight wring every bit of wisdom they can from the past, and they make deposits into the accounts from which great futures are built.

Experience plus reflection equals insight.

What might this look like in practice? Specifically, I know several people who set aside one day per calendar quarter to purposely spend time in solitude, prayer, Scripture reading, meditation, and journaling. They report that much good comes from these purposeful times of reflection. I know a Christian leader who regularly prays about items of concern for a calculated amount of time, usually forty days, to gain God's perspective on major decisions and life's priorities. I know a woman who regularly fasts as she seeks the Lord's direction. She advocates "alone time with God" as the necessary precursor to moving forward.

These methods of reflecting are all helpful, for experience without reflection can rush us toward false conclusions. A lack of reflection can cause us to become jaded or at least fearful to try again. We choose to live cautiously rather than become fully engaged. Mark Twain once said, "A cat that sits on a hot stove not only will never sit on a hot stove again, it won't sit on any stove!"[4] That becomes our default way of living. A life of fear is based on the avoidance of action, but a life of faith is based on trust in God's guidance and action. An irresistible church takes the time to reflect on God's ways and, in doing so, learns to follow them.

One of the specific ways we reflect on lessons at New Hope Oahu is by holding specific leadership meetings we call *debriefings*. Over the years, we have aimed to build a culture of consistent learning by evaluating in these meetings. Note that I didn't say *criticizing* or *fault finding*. Debriefing is for the sake of improving by the lessons learned. For instance, each Saturday night after our first service is held, we bring key leaders into the back room and ask specific questions based on the purpose of the service.

This practice can be implemented in any size church. Some with one Sunday service debrief on Monday or Tuesday mornings. The closer the debriefing is to the completed service, the better—that's when your memory and recall are still fresh. I also do this with my family or a ministry project. Debriefing creates a metric by which we can begin to learn, improve, and often celebrate.

Questions we might ask include:

- Were people involved in the service? Were they participants or just spectators?
- Did we sense the movement of the Holy Spirit in the service, or were we simply going through the motions?
- Did the message grab both minds and hearts?
- Did anyone receive Christ?
- Did the service promote Jesus, or simply make us sound good?
- When people left, were they talking about Christ?
- What can we celebrate?

Notice the questions are not based on *preference*—what we liked and didn't like. The questions are always based on *purpose*. They ratchet us back to our mission, why we're doing what we do.

Also, we draw a line in our debriefing sessions between healthy discussion and argument. Discussion allows for differing opinions yet assumes we're on the same side. When we discuss things, we are trying to make better what God has told us to do. Argument, on the other hand, seeks dominance over another. A good leader and shepherd will not allow argument to generate in a meeting. We're all on the same team, and our goal is a greater measure of fruitfulness. After the questions have been asked, we make specific adjustments.

We give people who debrief the authority to honestly critique, yet it is always with the overarching goal of building up.

An irresistible church is always on mission. This means a church has never forgotten why she exists: to glorify God, to win people to Christ, and to equip the saints so that they do the work of ministry.

Well entrenched but ineffective

I have a friend who has worked with a rural camp ministry in Washington State. Over the years, camp administrators have sought to make various improvements and upgrades to the buildings and programs. But sometimes, even the most obvious changes needed are met with resistance from the camp's longtime constituency. For instance, several years ago the camp replaced its outhouses with flush toilets. Even this needed change drew criticism. Some apparently longed for the rusticity of the way things used to be.

Imagine getting nostalgic over outhouses!

Yet who hasn't made illogical complaints in our churches? Why, in our well-meaning Christian community, are we often so resistant to change?

Perhaps we can't bear the thought of selling the church bus. We have fond memories of its ministry, of the many grateful elderly people who were picked up and taken to church. Yet when we examine the church bus today, we can see that it is belching smoke and needs to be towed every time it's taken out on the highway! Service to shut-ins might be better served by using vans or by a videotape or Internet ministry. But we can't sell the bus—that would mean change.

Why, in our well-meaning Christian community, are we often so resistant to change?

Or maybe some can't bear the thought of not printing the order of service in the Sunday morning bulletin. There's always been a printed order of service and people are used to it. Of course it's very difficult for the leadership to make changes to the service after the bulletin is printed, because people then look at the bulletin and wonder what's going on. But there's no way we could dream of doing things a different way!

On Mother's Day we have held an early breakfast before the first service as a fund-raiser for the junior high ministry. Of course now the fund-raiser is ill attended, and very little money is raised. The junior high kids are sleep deprived and cranky and dropping dishes, but can we bear to kill the program?

Is it possible to cancel the evening service on Super Bowl Sunday even though very few people come to the service and the ones who do would rather be home watching the game? With a little ingenuity we could construct a simple yet effective outreach-oriented men's ministry during that time slot. But no evening service? We've never done things that way before.

If I have stepped on anyone's toes, please do not close this book out of frustration or anger. Stepping on toes is not my intention. I simply encourage you to ask honest questions about your church's effectiveness. Learning to face the truth, no matter how painful that might be, is one of the greatest principles for improving life. We cannot move forward unless we can be courageous enough to recognize truth.

Apply this principle to other areas of life, and see its reality there. For instance, if we cannot acknowledge that the job we have is the wrong one for us, we'll never be able to make the changes necessary in our current job or switch careers to another.

If we don't recognize that our marriage is struggling, we won't seek help or rectify the hurtful words that aggravate arguments.

If we can't see the truth that we are overweight, we won't do what it takes to get rid of old habits that led to our obesity.

The truth will set us free; but first, the truth might make us uncomfortable, even miserable. Yet holding on to falsehoods and not going forward are worse, thereby denying the truth.

An irresistible church courageously confronts the problems of ineffective ministries, but it also responds with mercy and grace. An irresistible church is mature enough to recognize the existence of deadwood in its programs and methods. The problems are confronted in the same way a world-class group of surgeons would evaluate an X-ray prior to surgery. The problem is discovered, and the way to best resolve it is agreed upon. Surgeons don't berate the patient nor do they blame genetics. Their goal is simply to rectify the trouble and restore the patient to health.

Learn from the bad as well as the good

We can learn from the most unlikely places. This is helpful to remember when we consider the imperfect nature of all churches. It is said of a preacher named John Wesley White that he can *listen* an ordinary sermon into a spiritual masterpiece. In other words, he puts the responsibility of learning on himself and not on anyone else. His example is ours to learn from. We do well anytime we develop a hunger to learn fresh insights and experience new things. We can discover new truths from bad teachers as well as good ones.

One young leader returned from a two-month intensive session on apologetics at a university. I queried him upon his return, "How were the classes?"

"Half of them were good and half were bad," he replied.

"I don't understand. What do you mean?"

"Well," he said, "half the teachers were interesting so I learned from them. But the other teachers were boring, so I didn't learn from them."

"No!" I said with a shout, trying to catch his attention. "You must learn from the bad as well as the good. If you only learn from the good, you will only learn half as much. But if you learn from the bad as well, you'll learn twice as much."

"How can you learn from the bad?" he said. "They bored me to death in the first three minutes."

"That's fantastic," I said excitedly. "Do you know the kind of skill it takes to bore someone to death within three minutes? Find out what he's doing to accomplish that feat. Write it down. Was it his monotone voice? Maybe he didn't know his subject matter. Perhaps he wandered from topic to topic. Or could it have been a lack of passion? Find out whatever it was, and you will know what *not* to do when you are asked to teach one day."

Always learning

Renew your commitment to fresh learning, no matter how long your church has been in existence. Develop people skills, organizational skills, logistics skills, and team skills, and learn how to resolve disputes. Hosea 4:6 says, "My people are destroyed from lack of knowledge." The implication, therefore, is that knowledge is valuable, something to be continually pursued. This is not the type of pride-filled knowledge mentioned in 1 Corinthians 8:1, where "knowledge puffs up." Rather, it is the knowledge found in Proverbs 1:1–7, a type of practical wisdom that enables us to develop a wise, skillful approach to living. This is knowledge based on God's virtues. It helps us become more loving, faithful, and hopeful, and to reach more people for the gospel.

Renew your commitment to fresh learning, no matter how long your church has been in existence.

Perhaps this new knowledge emerges in your church as:

- An administrative assistant learning a new computer program so she can design a better bulletin.

- An associate pastor going back to school to keep his credentials sharp or a teaching pastor taking a seminar to become a more effective communicator.
- Each member of a high school youth staff regularly attending national conferences to stay up-to-date with current trends in youth ministry.
- A worship team continually working on new songs, taking advanced music lessons, and honing their skills.
- An elder board studying books on effective church management.
- Small-group leaders regularly attending training sessions to learn how to facilitate group discussions.

You can always spot people in a church who have stopped learning. They become possessive and territorial. They say things like, "That's my desk, my stapler, my room, my closed group of friends, my area of the church." Why are they possessive and territorial? It's because they see new people coming into the church, and that's scary and intimidating to them. They want to cling to what they have rather than learn new skills to become people of excellence, thereby reflecting God's glory and helping to draw more people to Him.

Don't stop learning. Take the initiative to discover new truths about yourself and about God. Don't be afraid of honest reflection. What you'll find when you dig deeply will be the materials out of which great futures are made.

ACTION STEP: Resolve to always keep learning.

AN IRRESISTIBLE CHURCH PROMOTES SPIRITUAL SELF-FEEDING

The young associate pastor looked haggard when he entered my office. "I think my season here is up," he said.

I leaned back in my chair. "Why?"

"Well . . ." He hesitated. "I'm just not being *fed* here."

I had heard those words before from a few people who had left our church, but this time it had me bewildered. This man had been on staff with us for four years, and if there's one drum we beat on incessantly in our work culture around here, it's the necessity of having a daily devotional time. I knew that this staff person was neglecting one of the most important aspects of genuine Christian maturity.

"Not getting *fed*?" I pressed. "Tell me. Are you regularly spending time alone with God?"

"I don't have time," he said. "I'm too busy."

"How old are you?"

"Twenty-eight."

"That's my son's age. Let me pose a scenario to you. What if my son came to me one day looking gaunt and emaciated? His eyes are sunken, his body is frail, and his ribs are showing. Now let's say he gives me a depressed look and says, 'I'm leaving this family.' I respond, 'Why in the world would you do that?' He says, 'Because no one is feeding me around here anymore,' What do you think I would say to that?"

The man slumped in his chair. "Feed yourself?" he said.

This man knew the truth. He'd known it all along, but for some reason, he didn't feel it was necessary to follow the instruction . . . until it was too late. I accepted his resignation.

I don't mean for this story to sound harsh. The staff member wanted to resign, and a few other factors were in the mix in addition to his complaint of not being fed. So I didn't try to stop him. For the most part, I identified with him because I remembered a time when I was in the same place.

I remembered that shortly after I became a Christian, I complained to God about the quality of my church's teaching. We had an academic-style preacher who often left me more confused than anything else. After one Sunday morning service, I went to a bathroom stall, put the seat down and sat, fully clothed, with my head in my hands. "God!" I cried out, "I'm going to *starve* in this place! I'm not getting fed. I'm *dying*."

Water dripped from a faucet. An air-conditioning vent hummed a smooth murmur. I listened, hoping to hear the voice of God, then continued to intersperse my prayer with moments of silence, slowly becoming acutely conscious of the Holy Spirit's presence. There, finally, in that bathroom stall, words came to me as from the lips of God: *"Am I not enough?"*

I believe that was God's message to me at that time—*Am I not enough?* It was a gentle rebuke that meant I had been resisting God's best program, His most gifted teacher, the Holy Spirit. He had been inviting me to be His student, but I remained unresponsive. Instead, I wanted others to do what only I could do . . . take responsibility for my own spiritual health and nourishment. I had been trying to live off a once-a-week feeding regimen. No wonder I was starving.

The next day I began a Bible reading, prayer, and journaling program that is still with me. I have refined it over time, yet the same heart and motive remains: I alone am answerable for my spiritual maturity. In order to grow, I have to *feed myself.*

Water, even without thirst

The seventh trait of an irresistible church, a church God loves to bless, is that it is filled with self-feeders. Feeding ourselves is no one else's responsibility except our own. I cannot expect others to feed me. If I am to grow and mature, it is not the responsibility of a pastor, an elder, or a Sunday school teacher. Certainly these people will help coach me, instruct me, encourage me, and sharpen my skills; but I alone am responsible to feed *me.*

Feeding ourselves is
no one else's responsibility except our own.

We often don't take the maintenance of our souls seriously until it is too late. Years ago in school I trained for a long-distance race. My coach instructed me to hydrate at specified time intervals whether I felt like it or not. Every fifteen minutes I was to drink six ounces of water, and I was to keep an eye on the time so I didn't violate my hydration limits.

"But, coach," I asked, "what if I'm not thirsty?"

"Listen to me," he said with a serious stare. "If you wait until you're thirsty to take a drink, *it's too late.* Your body has already begun its slide into dehydration. You can't afford to wait."

Psalm 46:10 encourages this direction in the spirit realm. This passage offers us a wonderful invitation to self-feeding—and also a wonderful method. It says simply, "Be still, and know that I am God." The invitation is found in the second part of that short verse: to know God. The method is found in the first part of the verse: to be still.

An important part of being still is *solitude.* It's one of the vital keys to knowing God. Solitude renews a fatigued heart, and being alone with God is where a chafed soul goes to heal. Solitude provides the opportunity to scrub our souls and recalibrate life's compass. Without it, we can easily drift toward a chaotic, unexamined life, a life of spiritual starvation.

Solitude differs from isolation. The latter happens when we violate the former. If we don't have enough true solitude in our lives, we hunger to be left alone, often from the relationships that are most healthy: those with our closest friends, our spouse, and the Lord. We isolate ourselves whenever we try to feed our souls with the escapism of TV, the noise of the radio, or the busyness of our schedules, always desperately hoping for our discontent to pass. After we isolate ourselves in this manner we return to our healthy relationships unfulfilled.

Mother Teresa once said, "In order to keep a lamp burning, we have to keep putting oil in it." The oil we must fill our lamps with is the true oil of solitude with God. This oil maintains our hearts. It refreshes and invigorates us, offering us a renewed perspective for each new day, task, and challenge.

Come prepared to play soccer

Psalm 119:32–35 offers us additional insight into the self-feeding process. These verses point us to vast benefits, and invite us to be intrinsically motivated to regularly meet with the Lord:

> I run in the path of your commands,
> for you have set my heart free.
> Teach me, O Lord, to follow your decrees;
> then I will keep them to the end.

Give me understanding, and I will keep your law
and obey it with all my heart.
Direct me in the path of your commands,
for there I find delight.

Note the first verse of that passage. Why might we run in the path of God's commands? It's because God *sets our hearts free.* Our times of regular self-feeding never need to be times of drudgery or mere duty. God is a person who invites us to have a relationship with Him. His Word, the Bible, is living and active (Hebrews 4:12). When we follow His commands and precepts, the results are goodness, joy, and adventure.

Our times of regular self-feeding never need to be times of drudgery or mere duty.

In my early twenties I coached soccer at a nearby high school. The team enjoyed several successful years in a row and comprised a capable, winning group of young athletes. Students felt proud to be on this team, and the players who tried out for the team were already motivated. When they arrived for practice, even on the first day of a new season, they came to the field already suited up and ready to go.

One student, however, showed up on the first day of a new season wearing jeans and a backpack. "I'm not really sure if I want to play soccer," he said. "I think I might want to go out for band instead. What do you think, coach?"

"Well," I said slowly, "it sounds to me like you're leaning toward band."

He raised his eyebrows, unsure of where I was going with this.

"My main job is to help you play soccer," I continued, "not help you make decisions. Once your decision is made, I can increase your skill level and teach you patterns of play. But until you make your decision about which pathway to follow, I'm on the sidelines. If you choose to play soccer, I expect you to arrive already motivated for the game. So if you haven't made that decision yet, I can't coach you any further. Those of us here today have come already prepared to play soccer."

It was a strong truth, but I felt the lesson would stick with him more powerfully if I didn't waffle around in my language. The lesson was that successful team players arrive already motivated and coachable.

To apply the above illustration to church, self-feeders don't show up wearing blue jeans and a backpack. Self-feeders arrive at church wearing their soccer uniforms. I'm speaking metaphorically, of course. It means that people arrive having already made a decision to play ball. They have motivated themselves to hear God on a daily basis, and are already in that frame of mind when they walk through the front door. The weekend services help coach them further.

Think about it this way. In a recent edition of *The American Journal of Medicine*, doctors published a highly revealing conclusion: The health of twenty-first-century America will no longer be determined by what people can get the doctors to do for them. The health of America today will be determined by what the doctors can get people *to do for themselves*.[1] Can you see how this prescription applies equally to each of us? A once-a-week meal of braised skinless chicken, steamed vegetables, and a vitamin pill, no matter how healthy or scrumptious it might be, would in the long run still leave us weak and under-nourished if that's all we ate.

Self-feeders have motivated themselves to hear
God on a daily basis, and are already in that frame of
mind when they walk through the front door.

But daily meals can change all of that. Regularly dining on the Word of God makes for stalwart, healthy saints—the only kind that will make a difference in this world.

The responsibility—and the joy—of self-feeding is ours. In the passage from the Psalms that we read earlier, God invites us to *run in the path of His commands, for He sets our hearts free.* Our job, therefore, is to stretch, lace up our running shoes, and earnestly head out on the trail, prepared for the good things that lie ahead.

Unshaken

When we regularly feed on God's Word, it helps us know the Shepherd intimately. Our life takes on a stable, constant cadence where even though the storms threaten and assail us, we remain trusting in God's goodness, steadfast and unmovable. When we choose to be self-feeders, the words of Psalm 16:8 ring true to us each day: "I have set the Lord always before me. Because he is at my right hand, I will not be shaken."

A story is told of a talent show held in a small country church many years ago. Two performances stood out in people's minds that evening; the first was a visitor from the city. He was a seasoned professional actor, well trained in the Shakespearean tradition. Stepping up front, he cleared his throat, and in a deep, resonant voice, the Twenty-third Psalm echoed throughout the chapel. The actor recited the classic psalm with sweeping gestures, masterful poise, and flattering eloquence. He concluded to the brisk applause of a thrilled audience.

The pastor let a moment pass as a brief afterglow ensued. Then the pastor nodded his head toward a farmer near the back door. "Joseph, would you be next?" the pastor said.

"Aw shucks," the farmer replied. "I don't know nuthin'."

"Sure you do," the pastor said. "Come on up, Joseph."

Others joined in the coaxing until sheer embarrassment forced the farmer forward. Fidgeting from side to side, he half mumbled, "Shucks,

I don't know much; but all I can think to do is quote the same psalm as this other man did. I'm not much one for reading, and it's the only one I ever learned by heart. I'm afraid this other man beat me to it."

"Well, share it again, then," the pastor encouraged, and soon others were echoing the request.

The farmer was in his early sixties. Hard times had fallen on his life and little farm but he remained godly and soft-spoken, a man who never complained. Swallowing hard, he stammered and started with his own paraphrase. "The Lord is my Shepherd and 'cause of that one thing, I figure I have everything I need." Detouring on a side route, he continued. "Y'all know that my dear wife died six years ago. When my Helen passed, I didn't think I could go on without her. But God never left me and He reminded me that I was gonna do just *fine.* He said He'd be there for the kids and me, and He was."

The farmer paused to remember which verse he was on, then continued. "He makes me lie down in green pastures. He leads me beside still streams. He restores my soul. He leads me . . ." The farmer paused as his thoughts were interrupted by yet another remembrance. "Y'all know that when the war broke out, my boys felt it right to join up. The day they left was the last day I saw them alive. I run the farm alone now. . . . But the Lord goes before me and prepares my table. I'm never truly alone. Not really. And when I don't think I have much left, my cup always overflows."

He concluded the Twenty-third Psalm: "Surely goodness and mercy will follow me and I look forward to dwelling in the house of the Lord, and I know it will be my home too, and my wife's and my boys' . . . forever."

Knowing about God and knowing Him personally
are galaxies apart.

Without anyone noticing, a profound silence had filled the room; the kind when a deep respect is the only response you can give. It's the kind of silence when you don't know what to do, so you don't do anything at all. Joseph sat down, and no one moved. Then, slowly, the professional actor made his way to the front again. Standing for a moment as if to find words appropriate enough to disturb the silence, he spoke: "I may know the Shepherd's Psalm, but this man—" he pointed at the farmer— "he knows the Shepherd, and that makes all the difference."

Knowing about God and knowing Him personally are galaxies apart. One might bring notoriety or even fame, but the other brings *depth*. Recognize the difference and choose well. That one decision will make all the difference.

ACTION STEP: Be a self-feeder.

AN IRRESISTIBLE CHURCH CONNECTS EVERYTHING TO A SOUL

The Bible indicates that heaven holds sights and sounds in store for us that will astound even our wildest imaginations and keep us in awe for all eternity. Personally, I know I can't wait to talk with King David in person or walk with Enoch. I want to meet the archangels Michael and Gabriel, and see how God created the heavens, constellations such as Orion and Pleiades, and other wonders such as a supernova and the aurora borealis. For the first million years or so, I'm sure we'll be starstruck and suspended in amazement by all those things that take our breath away. We'll be mesmerized by the streets of gold, the cherubim, seraphim, and the saints of old. And I'm sure we'll spend years catching up with loved ones we haven't seen since they passed.

But what will make our hearts beat out of our chests will be when the clouds roll back and a trumpet blast splits the heavens. The Lamb of God will receive the shouts and cries of the millions who have been redeemed. The Promised One will step through a stellar explosion that will cause even angels to shield their eyes from the brilliance.

I remember the old hymn whose verses ring:

> When we all get to heaven,
> what a day of rejoicing that will be!
> When we all see Jesus,
> we'll sing and shout the victory![1]

We'll see so many breathtaking sights and magnificent scenes that it will take us centuries even to get past the initial sensation. But of all the trillions of surprises, there's one thing we will never see again for all of eternity.

We will never see another non-Christian.

Right now, in this life, we have the only opportunity to usher people to the Forgiver. Our lifetime contains the only possibility for us to play an active part in God's plan of salvation for others. We have been invited to partner with the Redeemer to present the good news in creative ways to those who need Him the most.

We did it together

The eighth trait of an irresistible church, a church God loves to bless, is that it connects everything it does to a soul. That means every function of the church is connected to the mission of somehow, somewhere, saving the lost and helping people grow in the faith. A church is not simply a subculture with its own music, fashions, diets, and movies. We are asked to be a counterculture, and in order to be salt we must be that. We cannot settle for being a community of people who rally around a common cause. There's earnestness and purposefulness to our work because of eternal consequences. God invites us to love, serve, and obey Him, and part of the adventure of following Him means that we get to have a hand in helping people find their way to the Lord.

Early on in our ministry, we decided to place great emphasis on winning souls for Christ. We wanted to become a "harvest church," one that sees a great many people turn from despair and darkness to victory, strength, and confidence, based on the work of Jesus on the cross. Of all the noble activities we could be involved in, we wanted to be known for one thing: helping people find their way to the Savior. We may not be the best at hosting social events or church conferences, or having huge buildings with impressive budgets. But in the end what matters the most will be the souls that have been redeemed.

In the end what matters the most will be
the souls that have been redeemed.

In light of that, we deliberately created a culture that helps people connect everything to a soul. We do that without apology, and we do it in informal and formal ways. For instance, in the early years of New Hope, I remember talking with one of our wonderful volunteers who arrived early one morning to help set up. In those days, our loud-speakers were attached to stands. The speakers were then manually raised to an appropriate height so the sound could be projected over the heads of the congregation for optimum dispersion. Just as the volunteer was completing the task, I posed a simple question to him. "Do you know what you are doing?" I asked.

"I'm setting up a speaker," he said.

"Really?" I replied. "Is that all?"

"Yep, that's about it," he said. "I've been doing this each week for six months."

"What would you say if I told you that you were doing much more?"

Quizzically he turned to me and said, "Okay, now you've got me hooked, Pastor. Just what am I doing?"

"You are making it possible for a new person to hear the gospel clearly and without distraction probably for the first time in his life," I said. "Because of your efforts here, when that person responds positively to Christ . . . when he lifts his hand to say yes to God's offer of forgiveness and salvation, we will rejoice together. Why? Because I didn't lead him to Christ . . . *We did it together!*"

He broke into a huge grin. "I see what you mean."

"Thank you for your work in helping lead people to Christ." I held out my hand and we shook.

I left the auditorium and walked over to our children's section. There I found a young woman from our Pacific Rim Bible College. She was volunteering in the nursery as part of her work-study program.

"What are you doing?" I asked.

"Why, I'm changing a diaper," she replied. She studied me for a moment, thinking, then voiced her thoughts: "That's kind of a strange question, isn't it, Pastor? You've got kids. With a minimum of observation skills anyone can recognize what I am doing."

I pressed forward. "What if I told you you're not actually changing a diaper?"

She wrinkled her nose. "I can tell you I most certainly am."

"Nope," I said.

"Then you tell me, Pastor, just what I am doing," she said with a wry smile, knowing something was up but not quite knowing what.

"You are making it possible for a young mother to entrust her child into the care of another. And because of that, she is able to listen to the gospel without being distracted by the constant needs of her child. At the end of the service when a young mother opens her heart to God, I didn't lead her to Christ . . . *We did it together!*"

She smiled.

"Thank you for your work in helping lead people to Christ," I said. I held out my hand to shake, but she gave me a hug instead.

Every function connects

Have you ever deliberately looked at every function of your church through the grid of its mission? For instance:

- The picnics, camps, and barbecues planned at church are never simply ends in themselves. They are always a means to something far more eternal.
- A greeter who shakes hands with people as they walk in the front door is doing much more than saying hello. She's helping set a friendly and relaxed tone and atmosphere that prompts a person to be more receptive to the gospel.
- A church that organizes a baseball team and plays in the community is doing much more than simply playing baseball. It's connecting people to other Christians to help win souls to Christ.
- A youth program is more than simply a place for the young people within a church to hang out and have fun together. It's a place of intentional discipleship.
- The volunteer who makes coffee each Sunday morning is doing much more than preparing a beverage. He's helping warm a heart in preparation for hearing the gospel.

We often don't see the long line of Christians with whom a non-Christian has contact before a decision is eventually reached.

It's all related. No one person leads another to Christ. It may be that one person eventually prays with another, or directly shares the gospel message with another, or gives a salvation message where a person responds in faith. But we often don't see the long line of Christians with whom a non-Christian has contact before a decision is eventually reached. All steps along the way are important. The Great Commission found in Matthew 28:18–20 is a corporate calling as much as it is an individual one.

We must never miss our true purpose as Christians. We must never function as if our role is to convince the already-convinced over and over again. I think when the day comes for me to stand before God's throne in heaven, He will ask me one specific question. He will not ask me how big our choir was. He won't ask how popular our potlucks were, nor will He ask the size and budget of our building program. He will ask one important question: "How many of my children did you bring home with you?"

Now is our time. We won't have another chance at this life again. This is our run. An irresistible church never forgets her assignment. Our energies, our activities, our planning, and our actions must somehow, somewhere always be connected to a soul.

A pastor friend of mine was in a board meeting years ago when one of the main items on the agenda was whether or not they should install ashtrays near one of the entrance doors of the church.

Those opposed to the idea believed that a church sanctuary was a sacred place, and if ashtrays were placed near the door that would suggest to others that smoking was an acceptable practice. The emphasis was on keeping the church building tidy, honorable, and respectable.

Those in favor of the idea recognized that people in need of a Savior were coming to the church, and some of them smoked. The emphasis was on welcoming nonbelievers for the sake of helping them find Christ.

One line of reasoning connected things to a building.

One line of reasoning connected things to a soul.

Do you see the important difference?

The lifesaving station

An Episcopal priest named Dr. Theodore O. Wedel penned a short parable in 1953 that I believe the Lord has used mightily over the years to help Christians see the true function of a church. It's often been quoted, yet the theme of this parable is so important, I don't want us to forget its truth.

On a dangerous sea coast where shipwrecks often occur, there was once a crude little lifesaving station. The building was just a hut, and there was only one boat, but the few devoted members kept a constant watch over the sea, and with no thought for their own comfort went out day and night tirelessly searching for the lost. Some of those who were saved and various others in the surrounding area wanted to become associated with the station and gave of their time, money, and effort for the support of its work. New boats were bought and new crews trained. The little lifesaving station grew.

Some of the members of the lifesaving station were unhappy that the building was so crude and poorly equipped. They felt that a more comfortable place should be provided as the first refuge of those saved from the sea. They replaced the emergency cots with beds and put better furniture in the enlarged building.

Now the lifesaving station became a popular gathering place for its members, and they decorated it beautifully because they used it as a sort of club. Fewer members were now interested in going to sea on lifesaving missions, so they hired lifeboat crews to do this work. The lifesaving motif still prevailed in the club's decorations, and there was a liturgical lifeboat in the room where the club's initiations were held. About this time a large ship wrecked off the coast, and the hired crews brought in boatloads of cold, wet and half-drowned people. They were dirty and sick. The beautiful new club was in chaos. So the property committee immediately had a shower house built outside the club where victims of shipwrecks could be cleaned up before coming inside.

At the next meeting, there was a split among the club membership. Most of the members wanted to stop the club's lifesaving activities for being unpleasant and a hindrance to the normal social life of the club. Some members insisted upon lifesaving as their primary purpose and pointed out that they were still called a life-saving station. But they were finally voted down and told that if they wanted to save the lives of all the various kinds of people who were shipwrecked in those waters, they could begin their own lifesaving station. So they did.

As the years went by, the new station experienced the same changes that had occurred in the old. It evolved into a club, and yet another lifesaving station was founded. History continued to repeat itself, and if you visit that sea coast today, you will find a number of exclusive clubs along that shore. Shipwrecks are frequent in those waters, but most of the people drown.[2]

---

*Let us always connect everything to a soul,
and help people find their way to Christ.*

My encouragement to us all is to throw open the doors to our lifesaving stations. Let's keep a constant watch over the sea, and head out day and night to the open ocean, tirelessly searching for the lost. The church is a place to welcome those who need Christ most. Let us always connect everything to a soul, and help people find their way to Christ.

ACTION STEP: Connect everything to a soul.

AN IRRESISTIBLE CHURCH CHOOSES TO LOVE

You could call me biased when it comes to my love for the Hawaiian people and culture. I come from a long line of merged Portuguese, Japanese, and Hawaiian ancestries. My great-grandfather was a *luna,* or a foreman, in the Parker Ranch area in Waimea, where many years later Anna and I planted a church. We only have a black-and-white photograph of him in his plaid *palaka* shirt, which was typically worn by ranch hands.

Our services in Waimea were held on Sunday evenings for nearly two years, until we installed a full-time pastor. Anna and I would leave from Hilo on Sunday afternoons and drive along the Hamakua coastline. I remember the sweet smell, thick in the humid air, of the freshly harvested sugarcane. Some days I rode my motorcycle past patches of pungent ginger as it grew wild along the roadway. A lingering gauntlet of fragrance would scent the air for miles. Now, years later, these memories still accompany me whenever I travel down the same highway.

Hawaii's fresh floral air energizes a person. Its breathtaking natural beauty brings renewal. But the unique feature that brings a person back to the islands is the people. The warmth of the aloha spirit in the islanders wonderfully complements the islands' perfect temperatures. A unique blend of nationalities and languages creates a distinctive flavor all its own as East and West merge to propagate some of the most beautiful people on the globe.

I have come to love the people of these islands, yet much of that love was a choice. I didn't always live here. I received my education and early experience in ministry in the Pacific Northwest—and that area of the country is beautiful as well, but different. We chose to move back to Hawaii more than twenty-seven years ago. Several reasons worked against our homeward move, but it was a love for the island people that compelled us. And no matter where I travel, that love that met me when I first arrived has never left.

That love for people, even love for an area of the country, is mandatory for a church to succeed.

How would you gauge your church's love for its community?

Strength for the journey

The ninth trait of an irresistible church, a church God loves to bless, is that she loves the people in her community as well as her call to reach them.

Have you ever considered what a powerfully motivating force love is? I recall a cross-country coach who instilled in me the love for running many years ago. (I will have to admit that since then, my love has somewhat flagged!) Nevertheless, when I joined the team, I asked him what priorities were needed in order to run great races. Should I purchase good shoes? Should I pick up a nice pair of spandex running shorts? What about a sports watch with multiple functions?

"It's none of the above," he said. "Your first priority is simply this: *to love running.* Enjoy the outdoors. Run during an early morning sunrise or an evening's sunset. Breathe in the fresh air. Take a detour through a park you've never visited. If you run only to win events, you'll soon get tired of it, but if you run because you love running, you'll run, and run, and run."

When we love someone deeply we serve with a glad heart.

The same principle holds true for our Christian lives. Many factors exist that can motivate a person to serve Christ. Some of these other motivations (such as guilt) succeed mostly in creating frustration or a false sense of duty. But 2 Corinthians 5:14 shows us the most excellent way: "Christ's love compels us." The concept is both freeing and empowering. When we love someone deeply we serve with a glad heart. Our actions are characterized by a sustainable passion—one that does not flare up nor die down quickly.

This type of love is described in 1 Corinthians 13. It's characterized by patience, kindness, goodness, and service. One synonym for this type of love is *compassion*. It's a love that serves people in need, and is the type of love often shown by Christ. For instance, Matthew 20:30–34 (NASB) records this wonderful story:

> Two blind men sitting by the road, hearing that Jesus was passing by, cried out, "Lord, have mercy on us, Son of David!" The crowd sternly told them to be quiet, but they cried out all the more, "Lord, Son of David, have mercy on us!"
>
> And Jesus stopped and called them, and said, "What do you want Me to do for you?"
>
> They said to Him, "Lord, we want our eyes to be opened."
>
> *Moved with compassion*, Jesus touched their eyes; and immediately they regained their sight and followed Him.

Christ's compassion moved Him to perform a miracle. This outworking of love is a powerful force.

Start with love

What if you or your church doesn't have this type of love for its calling and community? What do you do then?

One day I received a call from a man who was considering relocating to Hawaii to start a new church. We set a time to meet for breakfast at one of our local hangouts, Sam Choy's, on Nimitz Highway. We sat down and ordered from the menu. I had my favorite: Portuguese sausage, eggs, and rice. He had oatmeal. I guess I should have too, but my diet didn't begin until the next day. We exchanged a few pleasantries and then he began: "I serve with a denomination that has no representative church in these islands," he said. "They are willing to invest a considerable amount of money to get one started, and they've asked me to move here and lead it. What do you think?"

"That was nice of them to be willing to invest so much money in a new church plant," I replied. "Let me ask you a question: Do you love the Asian and Polynesian people?"

"Oh, they've been given the nicest place on the globe to live, haven't they? You can't beat Hawaii! And my kids love the beaches."

"I agree wholeheartedly!" I said. Then I repeated, "But do you love the people?"

"Yes, I just love the way they gather in families on the weekends at the beach. Why, where I come from, we just hunker down for six months a year waiting for spring to arrive!"

Still I wasn't sure he understood what I was truly asking, so I again repeated: "But do you love the *people* here?" slowly emphasizing the word *people*.

"What do you mean?" he replied. I could sense he was wrestling with the question now.

"The people here deserve to be loved deeply," I said. "Do you know their customs? Do you know the history of the islands? Did you know they take naps in the park and sometimes stop in the middle of the street to talk with a friend they haven't seen in a while? Do you like *kimchi?* What about *poi?* Have you ever tasted *haupia?* Would you be willing to try some *lumpia?*"

He stared at me as if I were speaking a foreign language. "I'm sure I will like their food. Back home, we have a Chinese restaurant that we eat at sometimes."

I smiled, thought for a moment, then said, "We really don't need another church here." He gave me an incredulous look that made me hasten to my next point. "But we can use many more Christian leaders who will choose to love Hawaii's people. Here's my take, for what it's worth: Don't start a church just yet. First, put up a map of Hawaii on your wall and pray over the towns; walk down the avenues, and learn how to pronounce the street names. Take some time to get to know the people. Learn to love them for who they are. Love the foods they eat, the customs they practice, and the way they live. The only reason to come to Hawaii must be to love the people in Christ's name; not for a job, not to fulfill a denomination's expectations, not for the weather. But if you'll come to love them, they'll come to love you."

My advice was too little—too late. The gears had already been in motion, and two months later he moved to Hawaii. He did his best to comply with his denomination's request. Three years later, however, the doors of the fledgling church were shut, and the pastor used the second leg of his round trip ticket back to the mainland.

Walking the map

A church must minister out of love—love of Christ first, and love for its community second. This mandate parallels the teachings of Christ. Matthew 22:35–40 records the story. An expert in the law asked Jesus what was the greatest commandment. Jesus replied: " 'Love the Lord your God with all your heart and with all your soul and with all your mind.' This is the first and greatest commandment. And the second is like it: 'Love your neighbor as yourself.' All the Law and the Prophets hang on these two commandments."

Love God.

Love others.

A church must minister out of love—love of Christ first, and love for its community second.

Simple truths, yet all else hinges on this. If a person merely attends church because he wants a safe place for his family to learn about God, or ministers to his neighbor because a pastor told him to, or serves food to homeless people because he senses an inequity in the world's distribution of resources, or attends youth group because he wants a fun place to go while his parents attend the church services, then that action or ministry will almost always wane over time. The greatest—and most sustainable—motivation for ministry must be love. We must serve because we love God and love others. Without love, we won't have the sustained impetus, strength, or energy to risk over the long haul.

This is true in many areas of our life. Think of it this way: If you love an activity, you have the time and energy for it. For instance, the other day I was relaxing on the couch at home after a long day of work. I felt so tired I couldn't move. Then all of a sudden I thought, *I haven't ridden my motorcycle for a few weeks. I'm going to go for a ride around the lake.* With renewed motivation, I sprang off the couch and went for a ride. I found the energy because I love riding my motorcycle, and my love for riding trumped my desire to enjoy the couch.

Before I went to Honolulu to plant a church there, I actually followed the advice I would one day give to the denominational church planter I had breakfast with. I put a 5- by 10-foot map on my office wall. Every day for six months I stood in front of that map. In my mind, I'd walk down every street and pray for the people. I traced the streets with my finger until I began to weep for the people who lived in those areas. I didn't even know them, but I walked the streets of Honolulu even before I moved there. I saw the people, I saw their needs, imagined their pain, and felt their frustration. I'd stop at a place on the map, for instance, that read *County Housing,* and I'd pray over every person who had interaction with that dot on the map. In time, God gave me a real passion and empathy for what the people of that area were going through.

Genuine love transforms what we believe
into how we live.

Apply this principle to any area of your church. Let's ask ourselves some difficult questions:

- Do you attend your particular church because you genuinely love God and love the people there? Or are you seeking to get something out of the church?
- Do you minister in a specific area because you sense a deep love for Christ and for the people who are served by that ministry?
- Does love for Christ and love for people guide the decision makers and implementers in your church? Do you sense that various programs and ministries are based on love?

Genuine love monitors our hearts and checks our motives. It governs our actions and prunes what is hollow. It transforms what we believe into how we live. It closes the gap of inconsistency and holds us firmly accountable to live what we believe.

Please don't stop

I find that the older I get the more I want to do only the things I love to do. That doesn't mean I do little, or that I'm picky. It simply means that I want to pour more heart into everything I do. If I am called to do a project, I will pray that the Lord will give me a heart for it. Every other motive for service tends to leave me shallow and fatigued.

I do not mean to suggest that I ignore being obedient to God. Sometimes God calls us to serve out of love, and sometimes God gives us clear assignments and asks us to obey regardless. The biblical stories of Moses and Jonah both fit this profile. Moses was called to lead the children of Israel to the Promised Land, but he asked God to send someone else. Jonah was called to speak truth to the Ninevites, but he ran the other way instead. Eventually, both Moses and Jonah responded in obedience, but even then, both appeared to serve reluctantly. Surely there will be times like those where God tests our obedience.

Sometimes God gives us clear assignments and asks us to obey regardless.

If that characterizes your season of life right now, please know that you are not alone. You are surrounded by a great cloud of witnesses. Your obedience to God is a form of love, and God will sustain you for the season, however long He wants you there.

I serve the church I now serve out of love, yet there have been times when it seemed I served more out of obedience than anything else. Either way, God has sustained me. Sometimes the rewards are seen clearly, too. Several years ago, I received one of the best letters ever from someone in my congregation. It was sent anonymously, and although I may never know the author, I will always be grateful for the gift. It is framed in my office and reminds me daily that love converts a belief into a conviction and it transports what's in my heart to what's in my shoes. I present it here in tribute to everyone who serves the Lord out of love and obedience. Chances are you could write your name in the recipient's position of this letter as well.

Here's an excerpt:

> When you asked Jesus into your heart, *you invested in me.* When you answered yes to the call, you invested in me. When you decided to be loyal to your spouse, you invested in me. When you let God make victories out of your defeats, you invested in me. When you refused to compromise, you invested in me. For all the "me's" in the church around the world, thank you for continuing to give your life. Please don't stop. You are showing each of us how to do the same.

ACTION STEP: Pray for love, and then let God's love compel your ministry.

AN IRRESISTIBLE CHURCH TAKES RISKS

Have you ever wrestled with God when you sensed He wanted you to take a risk?

Some years ago when I was in Hilo, I felt the Lord tell me to start all over again. My first inclination was that I didn't want to. I was forty-two years old, I had been in Hilo for eleven years, and we had built a congregation there of more than two thousand from a handful of saints. My heart was with the people, location, and work we had been doing. I was deeply invested in Hilo. I had no intention of leaving.

For about a year I wrestled with God. I wondered if I was misconstruing His voice. Experience reminded me of the wisdom of exploring a message to ascertain its certainty, so I asked one of our elders for counsel. He advised me to press through to assurance. "If you find the message to be false, then good," he said. "It means you're staying. But if the message is true, then that's also good—because the kingdom will only benefit if you go plant a church elsewhere."

So I prayed, fasted, and read God's Word. I sought the counsel of wise Christians. I talked with my wife extensively. After about a year, the message was clear—it was the same message I had been hearing all along. I knew in my heart that God wanted me to travel 250 miles north and start again from the ground up. It would be another church plant, again called New Hope, but an entirely new work.

After I knew the message was certain, I wanted to share it with a wise board member, Marie, and her husband. They came to our house after church and were waiting for me in their car when I drove up. I went to Marie's side of the car, leaned in the window, and explained what was going on. Immediately she said, "No, you're not ready. You're hearing God prematurely. The church isn't ready to have you go yet." She was adamant. Then, almost as if she was struck by something invisible, she started to weep uncontrollably. I thought I had offended her and asked if I had. She shook her head and said, "My tears are not about you offending me. When I said those last words, immediately I sensed the Holy Spirit telling me that I was the one mistaken. He revealed that something big is about to happen, and that I should not stand in His way. You might see this move as taking a big risk, but heaven does not see it as a risk. Heaven sees it as faith. We will miss you, but we send you with our blessings."

Marie's words have stood in my mind for all these years afterward. Her interpretation was true and reassuring: Heaven defines the risks we take for the Lord as *faith*. We may see a risk as unsettling, perhaps frightening, but when we are deep in the center of God's will, even a risk is safe.

Heaven defines the risks we take for the Lord as *faith*.

Are you sensing the Lord's call to risk something for the sake of the gospel? Even if you are at a place of comfort, stability, and effectiveness in your life, change may be right around the corner. You may fear a new beginning, but if God is calling you to step forward, there is no safer path you can take.

Learning to walk

The tenth trait of an irresistible church, a church God loves to bless, is that it takes risks. A risk, in this sense, is when a church steps forward in faith to minister in new kingdom-building initiatives. She responds in obedience to the leading of God.

Risking something seldom feels good, particularly not initially. Whenever a church takes a risk, some congregants will find it disturbing, upsetting, even crazy. They wonder why anyone would want to disrupt comfort and stability. At first glance, their logic makes sense. They look around and see smoothness: The Sunday services are down pat, the offices and buildings are established, women's ministries holds a retreat each fall, and the youth group takes an annual mission trip to Mexico. Why would anyone want to upset the apple cart?

I liken the concept of taking risks to a baby taking her first steps. Picture for a moment a baby learning to walk. For some time, the baby has been learning to stand. She'll fall, then stand again, wobble, then fall, then stand. Finally the baby will feel safe and stable on her feet. But in order to make forward movement and actually walk, she has to disrupt her stance. What she worked so hard and long to gain, she must now risk by voluntarily unbalancing herself. Only then will it be possible to take the first step. That disruption of equilibrium for the sake of forward movement is necessary for growth. That baby might be happy for a long time simply standing in one place. But if that's all she ever did, she would never learn to walk.

The same is true for us. If a church does not choose to risk, a church will not grow. When we purposely disturb our comfort and stability for the sake of advancing the kingdom, spiritual growth occurs. A church that takes risks is a church that understands that faith is alive. Our calling is not to arrive at a destination of stability, but to travel a pathway of constant growth and transformation. In order to live by faith, we must be willing to disturb the equilibrium of our lives.

Following the Spirit's lead

Mind you, risk is never about haphazard movement or about promoting instability for the sake of activity. Risk must always be in response to the Holy Spirit's guidance—such as when the Holy Spirit says *expand*, or *reach this people group*, or *venture out using the vehicle of this program*, or *kill this program for the sake of greater spiritual impact*, or *know me more deeply than you ever have before*. Risk is always an act of discipleship, of loving, serving, worshiping, obeying, and following God.

How, then, do we discern the leading of God in these matters? Certainly, all risk-taking first must be in alignment with the principles found in God's Word. God will never call us to risk in an area where He has clearly established a boundary. For instance, God would not call a Christian to risk and marry a non-Christian as a form of evangelism, because 2 Corinthians 6:14 states a clear prohibitive guideline in this area. Likewise, God would never call a church to risk and teach that Jesus is not God or that God is evil, because the opposite teaching is found in Scripture.

Once a leading is confirmed as aligned with Scripture, the specific leading of the Holy Spirit is discerned intuitively. What does this type of intuition feel like? That's where the relationship with Christ comes into bearing. Sometimes the Holy Spirit moves us forward by allowing us to feel uncomfortable where we are. We sense restlessness with our current state or a longing for something more. Sometimes the Holy Spirit places within us a deep desire to work with a specific people group, region, or ministry. We have a heart to reach the homeless, or we long to minister in areas of social justice. Sometimes, unlikely events will occur in our lives that seem more than coincidental. We receive a phone call out of the blue while we were praying for that person, or a letter comes with the message and words we have just been praying about.

Some people are uncomfortable with the intuitive side of our relationship with God because it feels too subjective. They want a formula, a plan to follow, something that's guaranteed to work when buttons are pushed. Yet the Lord calls us to sense His presence intuitively in accordance with scriptural directives. He wants us to deeply connect with Him every single day. That's why our daily times of Bible reading, prayer, and reflection are indispensable as individuals, and also why regular times of corporate prayer and seeking the Lord's will as a church body are crucial. A risk-taking church must base her guidance on a genuine relationship with Christ.

Certainly not every risk we take for the Lord is guaranteed to turn out as we hope. But if we refuse to take risks, we will never know if God has spoken or led. Sometimes the results aren't what we expect because we have misinterpreted God's guidance. We are all still learning to hear God. If we move forward with a pure heart out of relationship with Christ, and we have not ascertained His guidance correctly, then two things happen: (1) God is still pleased with our actions because we moved forward with obedience, and (2) Romans 8:28 comes into play—God works for the good of those who love Him, who have been called according to His purpose. Other times, a different result may come because God's definition of success or effectiveness can look much different than how we imagined it. The key is faithfulness, not seeing a specific result.

A risk-taking church must base her guidance on
a genuine relationship with Christ.

Key steps to risk-taking

The specific process of risk for a church involves at least five key steps. Each step will help to turn risk into an *adventure*:

1. **Begin every risk with the word *imagine*.** As God begins to guide you in an area, allow yourself to see the possibility

of what could be. Allow the words of Ephesians 3:20 to fill your heart. God says He can "do immeasurably more than all we ask or imagine." Never start with how fearful something will be, or how much it will cost, or who may or may not buy into it, or what people will think—those are all dream-killers, things that destroy our faith and make us become reticent to risk. Rather, start by dreaming big—*imagine what my family could be, my marriage could be, this Sunday school class could be*—dream up the best scenario you can. When we dream big, then God can say, *Good, I'm glad you imagined your most optimum scenario, because my dream is bigger still.*

2. **Shape the dream by seeing the potential.** Once a dream is imagined, the specifics of the dream begin to take shape. Often the person or church you are right now will not be able to accomplish a dream when it is really big. If the vision lies before you and it seems so big it's overwhelming, God says, "You're right—you can't do this on your own, but as you say yes to my plan for your life, I will grow and deepen you. As you accomplish this task, you will become a different person (or a different church)."

   Additionally, resources will be needed for that dream to become a reality. Look around and see what you already have. There may be potential in existing resources, including emerging leaders, a current program or ministry, a group of people needing something to do, contacts already established, financial streams yet untapped, or infrastructure that isn't being utilized. Start to pull together components that are already at your disposal.

   I encourage churches to try to do the will of God with the least dependency on money. Often a vision will be much greater than a bank account. The temptation is to reduce the vision. Rather, gather your imagination and innovation, take these ingredients, and become as resourceful as MacGyver. Look around your city. Who has the qualities or talents you need to fulfill the vision? Ask people, beg, borrow, and enlist. Pray that the Spirit of God will give you new vistas and horizons.

3. **Enlist a team of faith champions.** Visions are seldom accomplished alone. Because we're the body of Christ, I always bring a group of faith partners around a table to share the vision and bounce it off them. I want other people to own an idea rather than having it be mine alone. Plus, having people hear the voice of God corporately mitigates risk. I want to bring in people smarter than me so we can come to grips with the assignment before us. My recommendation is to select this group carefully. If something of faith is going to happen, we need to have faith champions around us. Avoid bringing dream-killers onto the team.

4. **Develop a bias for action.** Certainly there is wisdom in patience, prudence, and waiting on the Lord. Yet somewhere along the line, action must be taken. Seek the Lord's will, and then get going. James 2 states that action is a vital distinctive of faith. When a dream is imagined, people are prone to speak about it, talk about it, sing about it, pray about it, write songs about it, have conferences about it; but the temptation always exists not to move into action. For instance, we see this all the time when it comes to evangelism. We have conferences, seminars, classes, and advanced classes on evangelism, but we don't do it. When we complete all the classes, do we go out and evangelize? No, we become teachers leading the evangelism classes. Sooner or later, the bias for action must kick into gear—we say yes, take the risk, and throw our hearts over the line. Just go out and do it.

5. **Stay the course.** Reflection and reevaluation are necessary components of implementing any vision. Difficult seasons will come, seasons that tempt us to abandon a dream. Stay committed. Commitment is staying true to a worthy decision, long after the emotion of having made that decision has passed.

Sooner or later, the bias for action must kick into gear—we say yes, take the risk, and throw our hearts over the line.

Aim for a big harvest

A few years back, our church saw a need to minister to the inmates in Hawaii's prisons. We had no idea how to do this, and the thought of a prison ministry did not feel safe to us. But along with our observation of the need, we sensed God's calling in this area. So we began to pray.

Our services were being broadcast on the radio, and we had heard that a few inmates inside the prisons listened to the messages each week. Still, we did not know how to move beyond this. Our staffing and financial resources were busy elsewhere. But we continued to sense God's calling in this area, so we kept praying.

Over time, we heard that one of the inmates received Christ as a result of hearing our messages. His name was Roy Yamamoto. We met him. Nothing about Roy seemed safe at first. He was about 6 foot 4, weighed about 250 pounds, and was in prison for robbery, drugs, and collecting on gambling debts. Before he went to prison, Roy was a strong arm for bookies. He was the muscle, and he'd break people's arms as a way to motivate repayment.

When Roy was released after four years in prison, he began attending Sunday services at our church. He became an usher and did well at the job. Christ was truly changing his life. We still sensed that God wanted us to begin a prison ministry, so we decided to take a risk. I called a meeting with Roy and asked him if he'd like to start a ministry to inmates.

"Nah," he said, "I can't go out and minister. I sure couldn't lead a Bible study. Hey—I don't even *read*."

"What if we gave you a tutor to teach you to read the Bible?" I asked. "I'll bring you on staff so you'll have a salary in the meantime. Once you learn how to read, you can begin the ministry."

His eyes slowly lit up as he thought it over. "I think God would be real pleased by that," he said. "Let's give it a try."

We had no idea what would result. Few manuals on effective church leadership encourage churches to bring ex-cons on staff as pastors. But we did. We taught Roy to read, and he began the ministry to inmates.

The risk has resulted in an abundant harvest. Roy rose to the challenge. With the Lord's help, New Hope has a prison ministry today that extends to every prison in the state of Hawaii, as well as Arizona and Texas. Each year for the past several years, we have held a large summer camp for the children of incarcerated parents. At the camp, 80 percent of those kids turn their lives over to Christ. The warden in one of the prisons consented to broadcasting an hour-long video we made of the camp over the prison's internal broadcast system. He recently traveled to our church to share how much Roy's ministry has helped to change the culture of the inmates.

Many of our newest churches are planted in prisons. At the women's prison near our city, our Sunday services are so well attended they needed to go to two services. We recently held a fair for the children of incarcerated parents, and more than five thousand children attended.

I wish we could say all the risks we've taken have worked out like that. They haven't. But if I had to do it all over again and take a chance, I'd do this again in a heartbeat.

I find great comfort when I turn to Matthew 13 and read the

parable of the sower. The sower heads out to the field, intending to sow a large crop. He scatters seed on the soil and some lands on the path, some lands on shallow soil, some on weedy soil, and some on good ground. Time passes, and when he reaps the crop, only one out of the four soils produces.

If we want a big harvest tomorrow, we've got to scatter tons of seed today.

The principle is that whenever we sow spiritual seeds in people's lives, three out of four attempts won't yield the crop we hope for. Those don't seem like very good odds, but the good news is that the Bible also tells us that the small percentage of the crop that flourishes more than makes up for the loss. Mark 4:20 says, "Others, like seed sown on good soil, hear the word, accept it, and produce a crop—thirty, sixty or even a hundred times what was sown."

As Christians, our call is to sow lots of seed and take lots of risks. I often remind our leaders and volunteers that if we want a big harvest tomorrow, we've got to scatter tons of seed today. Not all of the ground will produce, so we don't want to conserve seed. We're aiming for a big harvest, so we want to risk big.

ACTION STEP: Step out on a risk.

AN IRRESISTIBLE CHURCH HUMBLES ITSELF

The new youth pastor could scarcely believe his ears. He'd only been on the job for two weeks, and already his senior pastor was buzzing him on the intercom, asking him to come down to his office and help out with "a special assignment."

The youth pastor wondered what the special assignment was going to be. He'd just graduated from seminary and was eager to put his newfound skills to work. Did the senior pastor need help with preparing his sermon? Perhaps they were going to parse some Greek verbs together. Maybe the pastor needed help with some large-scale all-church project he was working on.

With a gleeful grin, the youth pastor hurried down the long hallway to the other end of the church, where the pastor's office was located. But when he got there, he found the senior pastor with his raincoat on, a shovel in one hand, a garbage can in the other.

"What's going on?" the youth pastor asked.

"Got a coat?" the pastor said. "I should have told you to bring one. Every time it rains, the drain in the parking lot backs up. I need your help to hold the garbage can. We need to shovel out the sludge."

Welcome to following Christ. It's not about glory. It's not about applause. The chief end of man is to glorify God and enjoy Him forever. Sometimes that means finding joy in rolling up our sleeves and doing whatever jobs need to be done.

The vital assignment

The eleventh trait of an irresistible church, a church God loves to bless, is humility. This characteristic is demonstrated when a church follows the teaching found in James 4:10 and humbles itself so the Lord can lift it up in due time. This teaching is also found in 1 Peter 5:5–6: "God opposes the proud but gives grace to the humble. Humble yourselves, therefore, under God's mighty hand, that he may lift you up in due time."

Humility is remembering who we are in light of who God is. As Christians, we have a vital assignment that we don't want to miss. It's easy to get caught up in many things and miss what we're supposed to be about. But we are called to serve God and called to pour our lives into significant matters. Sometimes what is significant can surprise us. Matthew 10:42 says that even a cup of cold water given in Jesus' name can be significant. Our invitation is to represent and radiate Christ, to be an ambassador for Him, to think what He thinks, and to speak what He speaks. Our calling is to serve God in any way He asks.

Pride distracts

The Bible says in John 10:10 that the devil is intent upon destroying us. One of the prime ways he tries to destroy us is by distracting us. If our eyes get focused on the delicacies of sin, we are much less likely to fill our souls with Christ, the true Bread of Life, and it's easy to become distracted from our calling. A story is told of a centipede traveling down the road. A mouse scooted up beside him and said, "Hey, you have so many legs, how do you know which foot to put in front of which?" "You know, I never thought of that," the centipede said. As he began to consider all the possibilities, it distracted him so much he couldn't move forward. He didn't know which leg came first, second, or third.

Humility keeps us from being distracted
and missing our main assignment.

The same can be true for us. Humility keeps us from being distracted and missing our main assignment. The opposite of humility is pride. Pride entangles our feet so we don't know how to walk. It rears its head whenever our attitude about ourselves, positions, possessions, or accomplishments goes beyond justifiable self-respect.

Certainly, a healthy type of pride can exist—it's not wrong, for instance, to be proud of our heritage, or our daughter's soccer team. Yet pride becomes sin when we think of ourselves as better than we are, or start believing we're the ones ultimately responsible for our success, or when we simply focus on ourselves as the center of the universe. This dangerous kind of pride can be insidious when found in our churches.

Pride can take the form of entitlement, when we believe we deserve a certain success. It can take the form of overconfidence. It can subtly segue into an air of superiority where we begin to feel bulletproof. With a few successes under our belts, we can begin to think that whatever way we view a situation is the right way without question. It's easy to slide down the slope of unaccountability and aversion to correction.

On the other hand, humility is not about berating ourselves. It's about serving and exalting Christ. Practically speaking, humility comes when we discover that our greatest joy is in giving life away. Reward is not our applause, but rather the knowledge that we were able to serve Christ. This kind of humility is not gained easily. But it can be gained intentionally. The reason? Humility is not natural for us as humans.

In order for it to be developed, acts of humility must be intentionally planned, then carried out consistently until they become natural.

Humility comes when we discover
that our greatest joy is in giving life away.

Let's take a closer look at three ways humility can become an integral part of our churches.

Acts of hidden service

One of the simplest ways to develop humility is by consciously doing acts of hidden service. In the eyes of God, there is something very healthy about doing an act of kindness and not taking credit for it. An act of quiet kindness is an act of partnering with God. We do the service, and then God can use it in people's hearts for life change. I think of the progression this way: Good deeds bring goodwill that one day enables people to be open to the good news. There are no accolades or trumpets, no ticker tape parades. Yet we can take joy in the simple fact that we get to do good. It's like laying hands on a blind person and praying for him, and just before his eyes are opened, you disappear around the corner. The recipient would never know who it was who prayed for him. The only thing he'd know was that it was Jesus who healed him.

Humility.

In Matthew 6, Jesus said it this way:

Be careful not to do your "acts of righteousness" before men, to be seen by them. If you do, you will have no reward from your Father in heaven. So when you give to the needy, do not announce it with trumpets, as the hypocrites do in the synagogues and on the streets, to be honored by men. I tell you the truth, they have received their reward in full. But when you give to the needy, do not let your left hand know what your right hand is doing, so that your giving may be in secret. Then your Father, who sees what is done in secret, will reward you.

If we blow a trumpet about what we're doing, that's as far as that act is going to go. But when we do acts of service in secret, we will see far greater results come to pass as we do our part and then let God do His. Hidden service is healthy for our soul. Something of God's DNA begins to surface whenever we give without any strings attached and discover the joy of being God's messenger. When we intentionally do silent good deeds in His name, humility starts to become a natural part of us rather than a contrived Christian duty.

Now it's time for true confessions. Here's a pet peeve of mine: I hate seeing rubbish dumped on the road. One time in Hilo, I was driving to church and on the side of the highway lay a bunch of trash. The trash looked particularly bad because it had rained the night before. Beer cups were scattered all over the road.

When we do acts of service in secret,
we will see far greater results come to pass as
we do our part and then let God do His.

As I passed by I grumbled to myself about how the county needed to clean things up. I drove to church, preached for the first service, and then because we had only one car in those days, I drove home again to get my wife. On the way back home, I passed by the trash again, and I grumbled to myself again about "how inconsiderate people were." I got my wife and we drove up the highway, through the trash once again, still complaining and now telling her all about it: "Look at this; isn't it terrible?" I said. I preached again, drove home, and of course saw the trash again.

When I got home I was still grumbling.

Then, quietly, I heard God say, "Why don't you go clean it up?"

"Wait a minute," I said, "they don't pay me to do this."

I heard it again, "Why don't you just go clean it up yourself?"

I've lived long enough to know that when God says something to you, and you know it's God, you can't run from it. So I put a couple of black plastic garbage bags in my trunk. All I said to my wife was, "I've got to run an errand." It wasn't lying—it was an errand for God.

I drove my car back to the rubbish and parked behind some bushes. I didn't want anybody to see me. I waited for a lull in traffic, ran to the trash, and got busy stuffing the mess into the bags. Whenever a car passed, I ducked down. I didn't want anyone to think this trash was mine. Finally I got everything picked up, tied it up, and threw it in the back of my car. Then I drove over to a landfill to dump the bags. When I got home I washed my hands.

I didn't tell anyone about the incident. My silence wasn't out of pure motives—I was more embarrassed than anything. Soon I forgot about it. But the next Sunday I went to church and a couple stopped me in the lobby. They were new to the church but I guess they knew me from around town, because they said, "Pastor, the reason we came to church was because we saw you last week."

"Where?" I asked, thinking it might have been in a coffee shop I frequent.

"We saw you on the road picking up garbage," said the man. "We knew that if you were willing to stop and clean up something that wasn't yours, if you took the time to do that, then we'd be fine at this church."

I just had to grin.

The Lord can use the simplest actions to draw people to himself.

Remembering our mission

A second way for a church to become humble is to consciously remind itself that a church has a mission to do, and it must never forget that mission.

One practical way of staying true to that mission is to consider each function of a church through the eyes of a person the church is trying to reach. In most cases, this will be a visitor. The problem is that churches often become focused on serving the needs of the regular attendees week after week. After a while, a church can fall into a rut of continually preaching to the choir, no matter what the ministry is.

A church has a mission to do,
and it must never forget that mission.

I heard of a church that has signs at the entrance to the parking lot asking visitors to turn on their hazard lights. Then they're directed to special visitor parking spaces and welcomed personally. What does your church do to welcome newcomers?

Take a look at these areas through the eyes of a visitor:

- If a family is brand-new in town, can they find your church easily in a phone book or on the Internet? Are service times clearly visible? Is a map available?

- If visitors pull up in your parking lot, are open parking stalls easy to find? Is the front door of the church clearly marked and easy to find from the parking lot?

- Are greeters or ushers stationed at all main entrance doors to help welcome guests and answer any questions they might have?

- Are all pertinent rooms such as childcare areas, restrooms, and the main auditorium marked with clear signage?

- Is each service conducted in such a way that visitors feel welcomed? If a person has a limited spiritual background, will he feel completely confused at what's going on?
- If a visitor wants more information after a service, will it be clear to the visitor how to get it?

Humility keeps us on track. It prevents us from adopting the faulty perspective that church is all about us. We've got a mission to do, and our churches must always keep in mind the focus of that mission.

The mission of a church, as mentioned in previous chapters, is never solely about getting people into the church. Yes, we do acknowledge the purpose of weekend services in the lives of people. But a church's main mission is to equip believers to serve God throughout each day. The main mission field lies outside the walls of the church.

What would working in that mission field look like? Perhaps it's as simple as . . .

- A man giving up his seat on the bus for an elderly woman who would like to sit down.
- A stranger paying for the groceries of a college student who discovers in the checkout line that his debit card has expired.
- A couple picnicking in the park who gives a plate of food to a homeless man.
- A man giving up his parking spot for a mom in a minivan who looks to be at her wits' end.
- A gift card being sent anonymously to someone who needs it.

Once people see the value in humbling themselves, doors are opened to greatness. God can use even the simplest acts of kindness to draw people to himself.

Once people see the value in humbling themselves, doors are opened to greatness.

How we handle credit

A third way to build humility is to examine how we handle credit. I'm not talking about financial credit, but the credit we are given when we do something good. It might be something our church has done in a community, or a good idea we've had that's been implemented elsewhere, or a particular accomplishment. How do we handle the response? The rule of thumb is that whenever credit is *given,* it's safe. But whenever credit is *taken,* or stolen, it's destructive.

A story about destructive credit is found in the last chapter of 1 Samuel and the first chapter of 2 Samuel. King Saul was defeated by the Philistines. Severely wounded, he'd rather be dead than allow the Philistines to find him still alive and torture him. He turned to his armor-bearer and ordered him to finalize his wish. But his armor-bearer was terrified and refused, so Saul took his own sword and fell on it.

Later, another young man came upon Saul's dead body with his regal accoutrements nearby. So he gathered his crown and bracelet with an idea in mind. He delivered them to David, figuring that bringing these articles of Saul's would yield a good position with the new administration. The young man fabricated a story and told David of Saul's fatal wounds and that he mercifully ended the king's life to protect him from the cruelty of the Philistines' capture. Secretly, this young man decided to take credit for something he didn't do, and it worked against him. David condemned him for daring to strike down the Lord's anointed.

The young man thought he would be a hero, but instead, stolen credit became the sentence of death.

Whenever credit is *given,* it's safe. But whenever
credit is *taken,* or stolen, it's destructive.

It can be similarly dangerous when we try to do that today. Perhaps our lives will not be at stake, but it is always better to give credit away rather than take it. Proverbs 27:2 says, "Let another praise you, and not your own mouth; someone else, and not your own lips."

It's safe to accept credit, but don't demand it. Receive gifts that affirm your value, but don't perform for them. Accept gratitude but don't require it. Your faithfulness will bring accolades, but the need for attention should not drive you.

Your church today

I think it would be easy for us to read this chapter and gloss over it quickly. *Us? Proud? Never!* Pride can be terribly difficult to see and often imperceptible, especially when it lies within ourselves.

Friends of mine who attend another church shared an experience they had. Pastor John[1] was a candidate for a senior pastor position at an established church on the West Coast. He was a competent, intelligent man with an excellent seminary education, good speaking and leadership skills, and a reputable track record of solid pastoral leadership.

The church flew him and his wife out twice from their home in the Midwest for extensive interviews. He preached on two Sundays and spoke in four adult Sunday school classes. He met with the key leaders in the church who questioned him about his philosophy of ministry and vision for the church. He met with various small groups and answered all questions with tact and sincerity. Everyone agreed he'd be a perfect fit.

Near the end of their time together, one of the church's key leaders stood up in a meeting and affirmed: "Pastor John, you're going to like it at this church. In fact, it's going to be a cakewalk for you. We've long ago worked out any issues we might have. We're a congregation composed mainly of mature believers."

Yet no more than four years later, the church was in shambles. First, a key elder confessed that he'd been having an extramarital affair. Four full-time staff members soon thereafter resigned. The building program was immediately halted when the congregation discovered that the church was deeply in debt. And within six months, more than half the people had left for other churches.

Some blamed Pastor John. He resigned and left for another church. Some blamed the small pocket of elders who maintained a tight grip on all church decisions. Some blamed the style of music. Others blamed the youth pastor. Others blamed a large church that opened down the street.

Yet I suspected another factor was at work. This factor could be traced back to the words the leader used at that final meeting before Pastor John was hired. Think about them carefully: *"It's going to be a cakewalk for you. We've long ago worked out any issues we might have. We're a congregation composed mainly of mature believers."*

Ask yourself:
How can our church truly remain a humble church?

"Let him who thinks he stands take heed lest he fall" (1 Corinthians 10:12 NKJV).

That is the common consequence. Have you ever considered what a powerfully destructive force pride can be? Ask yourself: How can our church truly remain a humble church? Do we have a keen sense of our mission? How can we ensure that we are not distracted from that mission?

My prayer is that all our churches would understand the power of humility. It catches the attention of heaven every time. There's no greater joy than watching God do His job after we've done ours.

ACTION STEP: Walk humbly.

AN IRRESISTIBLE CHURCH HAS A PLAN

Imagine that a contractor sets out to build a house. Many excellent resources are at his disposal, and he is able to gather a talented team around him that can pour concrete and frame walls and wire lights and plumb a septic system. The sincerity of the team is without question. All those involved earnestly desire to build the best house possible.

Thus, the construction crew begins building. Each morning they rise early and work hard, hour after hour. They take a short lunch break and get right back to their tasks, working long into each evening. No one can fault the crew's skills, dedication, or passion for the job. Day after day, a flurry of activity takes place. Hammers and saws are heard throughout the neighborhood. Brick after brick is mortared and stacked. Board upon board is nailed together.

But as the house progresses, a strange pall begins to cast itself over the neighborhood. People walk by the building site to stop and stare. It's not out of admiration. They point their fingers, laugh, and snap pictures. Some shake their heads and throw up their hands, aghast.

You see, as the house begins to take shape, the walls go every which way. Some rooms have no doors. Other rooms have stairs that lead to nowhere. There's a porch, but it's disjointed and no one can walk across it. There's a roof, but it covers only portions of the house.

What's the problem?

One key ingredient was missing from the start. The construction crew had begun building without knowing where they were going. Much activity had taken place, but it was directionless activity, subject to the whims of each crew member and the needs and effort of each moment.

They had zeal, talent, money, and a willing crew . . . but no blueprint.

The resulting house became a rambling eyesore. At best, it became something to be ignored. At worst, it became an unsafe structure, a nuisance to the neighborhood, even a threat to those who frequented its interior.

What was the missing ingredient?

A common blueprint that everyone could follow.

For lack of a plan

The twelfth trait of an irresistible church, a church God loves to bless, is that it has a plan. This kind of church has earnestly sought God's guidance, developed a blueprint from that guidance, and boldly stepped forward to implement the plan. This kind of church knows where it's going, or at least has a very good idea of its direction. But although this church has a plan in place, it also acknowledges that God can change the plan at any season. It has a plan, but it's a flexible plan.

"The mind of man plans his way, but the Lord directs his steps" (Proverbs 16:9 NASB).

Of course it will be God who directs, but what will He direct if we have no plans? It would be like traveling to a new place without a map or GPS.

The reasons for the lack of planning are myriad. Sometimes we don't plan because we believe it's not in our makeup. Other times, sheer negligence prompts a lack of planning. Other pursuits occupy each day and little heed is given to this endeavor. Sometimes we are simply too busy. People's schedules are too full for contemplation and strategizing.

> To plan is not wrong. To the contrary,
> it is commended scripturally.

I have also encountered those with whom the idea of planning feels like a waste of time, even unspiritual. These are well-meaning people who are sensitive to the Holy Spirit's leading, and who want to be led *only* by God. While this is admirable, they mistakenly conclude that God's leading does not allow them to make plans lest the origins of those plans lay in man's desires and not in God's. Fearful to plan at the risk of offending God, they somehow feel it more spiritual to move forward without a plan.

To plan or not to plan

Let's examine some of the biblical foundations behind planning. Scripture addresses the reasons that people fail to plan while also teaching the prudence of planning ahead as long as those plans acknowledge God's sovereignty. Indeed, the Bible teaches that it is honoring to formulate when we formulate a strategy for action based upon the knowledge received. This way we have a divine blueprint from which to build.

One passage that sometimes scares people away from planning is James 4:13–15:

> Now listen, you who say, "Today or tomorrow we will go to this or that city, spend a year there, carry on business and make money." Why, you do not even know what will happen tomorrow. . . . Instead, you ought to say, "If it is the Lord's will, we will live and do this or that."

141

People sometimes view this passage as a prohibition against planning. Yet a clear reading reveals that it actually prompts us to make plans, as far as our plans are guided by God. We are instructed to make plans by saying, "If it is the Lord's will . . ." and then not boast about our plans. The passage is not anti-planning. It is pro-planning and anti-pride.

Proverbs 16:3 says, "Commit to the Lord whatever you do, and *your plans will succeed.*" Proverbs 20:18 says, "*Make plans* by seeking advice." And Psalm 20:4 says, "May he give you the desire of your heart and *make all your plans succeed.*" Therefore, to plan is not wrong. To the contrary, it is commended scripturally.

Here is the balance. In Acts 16:6–7, the apostle Paul and his companions have made a plan to preach the gospel in Bithynia, but the Spirit of God does not allow them to go to this region, so they travel to Troas instead. Although Paul and his companions planned for a certain course of action, they were sensitive to the Lord's altering their plans. This is our invitation as well. The Lord invites us to use our minds, prayerfully organize our thoughts, chart out strategies, and set goals, yet we must always do so in humility, recognizing that God alone controls our destinies.

Early on, the Scripture that God impressed upon our hearts when we prayerfully planned our church was Jeremiah 29:11: " 'For I know the plans I have for you,' declares the Lord, 'plans to prosper you and not to harm you, plans to give you hope and a future.' "

We took the biblical principles found in that passage to mean that God has plans for our church's future. Since God has plans, then God desires for us to know those plans in His time and His way. We concluded logically that God would not keep His plans to himself. The key for us, then, was to ask the Lord what His plans were according to the promise of James 1:5 and then walk in obedience by carrying out those plans.

My heart and desire for you as you finish this book is that you would not take casually the future that lies ahead of you. Do you know where you're going? Do you have a blueprint? Have you begun to act upon that plan?

In the end, God will not hold us accountable for what we have done. *He will hold us accountable for how much we've done of what He asked us to do!*

So sit before God and write out the plans that you believe God has for you so that you can set your course in obedience.

Unprecedented opportunity

There's a vitally important reason why we would want our churches to have plans. The older I get the more my heart's desire is to see the greatest number of people possible yield their futures to the Lord Jesus, first by discerning what His plans are for them. Not knowing His plan is not a sufficient reason to do nothing.

My heart and desire for you also is that you would not take casually the future that lies ahead for your church.

We need to make plans because we are in an era of unprecedented spiritual opportunity. All across the globe, people are spiritually hungry. Scripture tells us that the fields are ripe for harvest (John 4:35), and our love of Christ can compel us forward to introduce great numbers of people to Him. Our churches need to strategize like the "men of Issachar, who understood the times and knew what [they] should do" (1 Chronicles 12:32).

_____

My heart and desire for you also
is that you would not take casually
the future that lies ahead for your church.

_____

143

Crisis time

Perhaps you're wondering how you could possibly see the immediate future as a time of unprecedented spiritual opportunity when your church is in the midst of a crisis or perhaps you're presently operating without effective leadership.

The main key is *perspective*.

Much of how we see opportunity depends on how we look at our circumstances, no matter what those circumstances are. For instance, at the time of this book's writing, we have just come through a season in North America that commentators have termed "The Great Recession." Unemployment rates are up. The deficit is sky-high. The prognosis for economic recovery still looks sluggish. Yet perspective allows us to turn the tables on this season of crisis and, as the insurance ad says, see it not as "The Great Recession" but rather "The Recession That Made Us Great."

Do you see the difference? A difficult season has a way of stripping away everything unnecessary. It brings us down to fighting weight. When in crisis, we jettison all superfluous activity, and only that which is most important remains. The next season certainly holds unprecedented opportunity for our churches, but we need to grasp the right way of perceiving our circumstances; otherwise we will miss the opportunity. A crisis can actually be used as a tool for good.

A crisis is a terrible thing to waste. It can make us great.

Your preferred future

I encourage your church to take time—more than five minutes—to plan out what you believe God has for your preferred future. How will you know? Start with a simple question: "What will God hold our church accountable for in that day?" And if we aimed to fulfill that, "What would our preferred future look like?"

I encourage your church to take time to plan out
what you believe God has for your preferred future.

As you imagine the best possible scenarios, ask yourself questions
like these:

- For what purpose does our church truly exist?
- What main demographic of people do we want to reach? Families? Senior citizens? Young couples? All ages? Urban groups? Suburban? Rural?
- What are we *able* to do well, and what are we *unable* to do well?
- What are the main areas to be emphasized in our church? For instance, are we a church that promotes strong preaching, an excellent youth ministry, an outreach ministry to the poor, a ministry to military families, acts of compassion within the city, a jail ministry, or [you fill in the blank]?
- Would we like to see marriages strengthened in this church? If so, what steps will we take?
- Do we hope to train up the next generation in this church? If so, what steps will we take?
- How do we hope to be a blessing to our city and immediate community?
- How do we hope to encourage a global perspective of faith and missions? How will we help Christians in other countries as they encourage the gospel?
- Five years from now, what do we hope this church will look like? Ten years from now?
- How is success defined for this church?

Make your own list. It is not my intention to offer a step-by-step outline for your church to progress. It is preferable that wise leaders in each church lead their congregation through intentional and fervent times of seeking heaven's guidance in accordance with the uniqueness of each local assembly. Draft a plan and put it on paper.

Pursue excellence

I would, however, like to offer one necessary framework that will help leaders work through the specifics of this endeavor. Think of this as an overall mindset to adopt. The framework: When developing a plan, it is crucial to adopt a biblical, optimistic philosophy. A philosophy, in this sense of the word, is our perception of life. Matthew 6:22–23 says, "The eye is the lamp of the body. If your eyes are good, your whole body will be full of light. But if your eyes are bad, your whole body will be full of darkness. If then the light within you is darkness, how great is that darkness!"

When developing a plan, it is crucial to adopt a biblical, optimistic philosophy.

As we discussed in chapter 4, much of life depends on how we perceive it. I do not mean to equate this principle with some forms of Eastern teaching that hold that substances exist only because they are true in our minds. Not at all. What I mean is that if we believe in a good God who redeems mankind from despair and darkness, then we should choose to live with the perspective of victory, strength, and confidence. That's what I mean by adopting a biblical, optimistic philosophy.

Too many Christians live under the belief that we remain as worms before God, even after our salvation. It is true that the Bible points to the depravity of man in his fallen state, and that our hearts without

Christ are deceitful above all things and beyond cure (Jeremiah 17:9). Yet Scripture also indicates that God invites us to become excellent people based on the work Christ has done on the cross. Christ is in the business of redemption and transformation, and Scripture indicates that God wants us to become people of excellence. For instance, Psalm 8:1 says, "O Jehovah, our Lord, How excellent is thy name in all the earth" (asv). If God's name depicts His character, then according to this passage we serve an excellent God. Second Corinthians 3:18 indicates we are "being transformed into *his likeness* with ever-increasing glory." Thus, if God created people in His image, then we should become an excellent people, and our churches should follow suit and become excellent churches.

Certainly churches have the power to go either way—toward excellence, or toward mediocrity, even failure. I'm reminded of an old axiom: *Life will not give you what you desire or even deserve. Life will give you what you settle for.*

As you develop a plan for your church and imagine your preferred future, remember that God is a God of excellence. Imagine a future in which your church has become the best it can be, a church of excellence.

Then make a plan for that dream to become reality.

The miracle piece

Do you want to know the miracle piece of having a plan?

Action.

If we don't have action, all we have are good intentions. We might have dreams, perhaps even plans, but unless there's action, those dreams will never materialize.

There's another word for action, a word we don't like as much. It's *work.* That's right. *Labor.*

Mothers need to go through labor pains in order to bring new life into the world. Our churches need to labor if we want to see our preferred future become reality. We must take our blueprints and put muscle to them. Certainly there is credence to having extended times of seeking the Lord's guidance, of having seasons of apprenticeship and planning, or waiting on the Lord until His will becomes clear. Yet somewhere, eventually, it is imperative that some action take place. Without action, a blueprint can sit untouched in a church's file cabinet for years. God wants our future to be about more than good intentions. He wants our future to materialize.

Our churches need to labor if we want to see our preferred future become reality.

Can you imagine a race where no course has been set? The runners gather at the starting line and the announcer calls, "On your mark, get set, go!" The runners dart off in every direction! Races like that would end up on *World's Craziest Videos*. But we do that all the time in our churches. We line up at the starting line, someone cracks the gun, and people head out in a rush without knowing where they're going. And the eternal consequences of what happens in and through a church are infinitely more important than a footrace.

Now can you imagine a race where there's a set course but no running ever takes place? The runners stand around at the starting point to talk about the race, speculate with sweeping gestures on how grand the race will be, even pre-congratulating themselves on one day winning such a fine footrace.

But they never actually run.

My hope is that we would never again think casually about our church's future. The more clearly a plan is developed and then implemented, the better we'll be able to chart a course in obedience and run in faith. The clearer the blueprint the better the outcome of the building. The more sharply focused our target, the more apt we will be to hit it. Results don't come from leisure; they come from labor.

Picture this

The next time you're in your church's sanctuary, take a good look around. How did it come to be? It's there because someone saw it clearly even when the ground upon which that building now sits was still a vacant lot. They imagined what the future could be, made plans, and worked toward those plans becoming a reality.

The next time someone is baptized in your church, ask how that baptism came to be. It will likely be because some seasons ago someone hoped his friend would come to know Christ. That person prayed, loved, and befriended the other person and eventually shared the gospel with him. The Holy Spirit quickened that person's heart and he turned his life over to Christ.

The next time a single mother is given a bag of groceries because of the kindness of a member of your church, or the next time an art fair is held in your community because church members want to honor God with their creativity, or the next time a man addicted to alcohol goes twelve months clean and sober thanks to a recovery program in your church, ask yourself how all those good things came to be.

It's because your church had a plan and then acted on that plan.

Art Linkletter, who was a great friend of Walt Disney, once shared a story that took place during the fiftieth anniversary of Disneyland, after the park's founder had passed away. A man said to Linkletter, "Isn't it a shame that Walt Disney couldn't be here to see all this?" and Art said, "He did see this. That's why it's here."[1]

Move forward

It's always going to be more difficult steering a parked car than it will be to steer one that is moving. And don't worry about plans morphing along the way. Plans, even imperfect ones, will give you forward impulsion.

A story is told of a young boy who was asked by his father to check on the animals in the barn before bedtime. His father lit a lantern and sent him on his way. The little boy stopped and lamented, "I'm afraid! This lantern only has enough light for one or two steps, and then it's dark." The wise father replied, "Just walk forward to the edge of your light, and when you do, the next step will be illuminated."

That's our invitation as irresistible churches: to prayerfully see what could be in order that it can be, and then walk to the edge of the light you have been given.

And the good news is this: If you are willing, you'll hear heaven's voice say, *Come. Let's walk down that road together.*

ACTION STEP: Make a plan.

Thank you so much for reading this book. My prayer is that all across the country, everyday churches will become irresistible churches—churches that are champions at leading people closer to God being conduits for the Holy Spirit to change lives for the better, and impacting society for good. Irresistible churches are blessings to God and blessings to us. When we find out who we are, and are fully settled on doing what God has asked us to do and be, then our days won't be wasted doing the wrong things. Our lives will be well stewarded.

To that aim, this portion of the book is dedicated to discussion questions and a Bible study. I want to help you think and talk through the ideas in *The Irresistible Church*. Please feel free to use this section either personally or in a group.

If you are a group leader, allow me to suggest some quick reminders:

- Encourage everyone in your group to read through *The Irresistible Church* in its entirety. You may want them to do this before you begin the study or read a chapter each week. Stay open to whatever questions they might have as a result of interacting with the content.
- As you lead the study, varied questions and opinions will undoubtedly arise. Whenever possible, go to the Scriptures

together to find God's answers and perspective. Keep God in charge of your discussions.

- Set an example of honesty by responding authentically to the themes of the book. Leaders are models of growth, not perfection, and we all have room to grow in learning how to live out the ideas presented here. I encourage you to be candid about your experiences, questions, and thoughts.

- Pray with and for your group members and for your church. Ask God to be at work in their lives, and thank Him ahead of time (by faith) for what He will do both in their lives individually and within your church.

- As you pray, ask God to protect your small group from disunity, self-seeking, and pride. Ask the Holy Spirit to give each of you spiritual insight into biblical truth, personal discoveries, and breakthroughs both in individuals and in your church body.

Trait 1: An Irresistible Church Hungers for the Presence of God

Remember the Big Idea

Often we are more interested in the logistics of a particular program, ministry, service, or other function of a church than in seeking the presence of God. Yet seeking the presence of God is of utmost importance. Our churches cannot survive without it.

Churches, being spiritual climates by nature, are often unwilling to acknowledge a lack of God's presence. Honest assessment is required in this area. If God's presence is not sensed in your church, take steps to move in this direction: (1) recognize the vacuum; (2) fill up the vacuum with what is righteous; and (3) purposely exhibit tangible, visible signs of the faith.

Study God's Word

1. This chapter prompts you to gauge "the vacuum"; i.e., a church's lack of God's presence. How is your church's health in this area—positive or negative?

2. Have you ever been more concerned about how a church is run than about experiencing God's presence? Explain.

3. Read Matthew 18:20; Jeremiah 23:24; and James 4:8. If God is already omnipresent, what does it mean to seek the presence of God?

4. Read Ephesians 5:18–20 and Galatians 5:22–23. According to these passages, when we are filled with the Holy Spirit, what traits will be evident in our lives? Give some practical examples of what these might look like.

5. Read Psalm 145:18 and Hebrews 12:1–2. What does it mean to call upon God in truth, and what practical actions can be taken to experience God's presence in a greater way?

6. As mentioned in this chapter, how can "painting a church's atmosphere with the colors of heaven" help align a church's heart with heaven? What must never be forgotten when undertaking this action step?

7. Share a time when you experienced God's presence. What happened?

Spend some time in prayer, asking God for a greater sense of His presence.

Trait 2: An Irresistible Church Remembers Who She Is

Remember the Big Idea

If we follow Christ, we are part of the body of believers that comprises the universal church. Our true identity is a glorious one, like a bride on her wedding day. This is an identity that positions us for action. The church is loved and chosen, empowered by God, and set apart for service. Our invitation is always to remember our true identity and then to act on that identity.

When we speak of the irresistible church, we mean a local assembly that people can't get enough of. Yet more important, it means that we've remembered our true identity as the bride of Christ and are living in light of that identity. Such a title means we're in the process of developing the traits that make us glorious as a bride. Ultimately, a church is irresistible because a church reflects Christ's glory—and Christ is the One who is truly irresistible.

Study God's Word

1. Why is it vitally important that we understand the true identity of the church, and then act upon that identity?

2. Read Revelation 21:9–10 and Ephesians 5:21–30. According to these passages, describe the relationship of Christ to the church.

3. Read 2 Timothy 2:3–4 and 1 Peter 2:9. How is the church's identity described in these passages?

4. On a scale of 1–10, with 1 being a forgotten identity and 10 being a remembered identity, how would you honestly evaluate your church's position?

5. Read Hebrews 10:23–25 and Philippians 2:14–16. Discuss the relationship between the "gathering" and "scattering" functions of a church as described in these passages. In other words, what are we called to do when we come together as a church for a Sunday service, and what are we called to do as a church the rest of the week?

6. Read Matthew 5:13–16. Give some practical examples of how we can be "salt" (a preservative in the midst of decay)

and "light" (illumination in darkness) both within the church (building) and apart from it during the course of the week.

7. List some practical ways your church can remember its true identity and act upon it.

Spend some time in prayer, asking the Lord to help your group understand its true identity as a church and how they can then act on that identity.

Trait 3: An Irresistible Church Lives Heart First

Remember the Big Idea

An irresistible church lives heart first. This is the opposite of living image first. It means working and serving God with true passion and living with an intrinsic desire to travel the pathways down which God leads and invites us to follow.

The danger comes when our programs outgrow our hearts. Usually in the beginning of any ministry-oriented initiative, we lead with our passion. We take more risks. We develop things with a sort of raw energy. Yet once a program is implemented, the temptation is to slip into autopilot. We sit back, thinking the program will continue to produce the same results. The problem is that our hearts start to depend on the program, with no heart behind it.

Living heart first does not come accidentally. It is produced and maintained by vigilant monitoring. The human tendency drifts toward selfishness and ease, and only through conscious, daily effort will we break free.

Study God's Word

1. What does it look like when a church lives heart first?

2. On a scale of 1–10, where would you place your church on living heart first?

3. Read 1 Peter 5:2. Describe the motivation for service found in this passage. What might this look like when lived out in your church?

4. Three characteristics of living heart first are described in this chapter: being quick to forgive; having a larger capacity to receive godly correction; and willingly living a surrendered life. Which trait is the most difficult for you, and why? Which trait is the most natural for you, and why?

5. Discuss the difference between a church program or ministry that's simply up and running and being maintained, and a program that is truly used as a conduit of life change and spiritual impact.

6. Living heart first means living with sustainable excellence. Read Philippians 4:8 and Mark 6:30–32. Describe what it means to live a passionately balanced life. What safeguards might we need to build into our lives to go the distance when serving the Lord?

7. Read 2 Timothy 4:5–8. What can our churches learn from Paul's example about living heart first as found in this passage?

Spend some time in prayer, asking God to help you live heart first.

Trait 4: An Irresistible Church Practices Gratefulness

Remember the Big Idea

The fourth trait of an irresistible church is gratefulness. Gratefulness differs from thankfulness. Both are essential. Thankfulness is the cordial response to a favor done. It is the affirmation we give when things go our way. It is the reply to a gift or a promotion; it's the hooray after a blessing.

Gratefulness, however, is different. It can only be developed intentionally. It begins with a spirit. It's an attitude, a disposition that we carry and practice whether or not things go our way. Gratefulness means being content before any gifts are given—or even if they're not given. It's breathing a silent thank-you regardless of our circumstances. Gratefulness is a hallelujah even when there's no guarantee of a blessing. It is the confidence to accept whatever God brings.

Study God's Word

1. On a scale of 1–10, with 10 being very grateful and 1 being not very grateful, how would you evaluate your own level of gratefulness and your church's level of gratefulness? Is there a connection between the two? Explain.

2. How can intentionally slowing ourselves down prompt us to become more grateful?

3. Read Philippians 4:8 and Matthew 6:22–23. How can these verses help us develop more gratefulness in our churches?

4. Read 1 Thessalonians 5:16–18. What is the difference between giving thanks *in the midst of every circumstance* and giving thanks *for* all circumstances? What does God call us to do?

5. Have you ever experienced a season where God said no to a prayer request but later you saw that it worked out for the best?

6. How can evaluating something according to its purpose (and not personal preference) contribute to gratefulness?

7. List five things about your church for which you are grateful.

Spend some time in prayer, simply thanking God for everything you can think of.

Trait 5: An Irresistible Church Promotes Healthy Relationships

Remember the Big Idea

When unresolved problems are tolerated in a church, the resulting unsettledness wreaks havoc on a local assembly like weeds on a plowed field. Visitors detect the inevitability of a bad crop even though they might not be able to pinpoint where its specific origins lie. Resolving conflict is paramount in a church, although it is seldom easy. But it can be done—on an ongoing basis—in your church as well as in mine.

Health emerges in a church when its members promote and encourage a sense of unity in the bond of love. Possessing this trait doesn't mean that everyone in a church always agrees with everyone else or that there are never any problems. It simply means that when problems do occur, we take the time and effort to resolve them in a timely manner. Ironically, it can be refreshing, even freeing, to acknowledge the inevitability of problems within a church. No church is problem-free, nor should we expect it to be. When we realize that problems commonly creep up in any local assembly, this releases us from the pressure of needing to have everything look tidy all the time.

Study God's Word

1. What factors can make it difficult or challenging for an organization to work through its conflict?

2. Read Proverbs 12:16. In what situations might it be prudent to overlook an insult?

3. Read Matthew 5:23–24. The principle in this passage is that having right relationships with people is more important

than outward spiritual practices. Describe some ways that this passage might apply to our lives.

4. Are there any reasons why it might actually be healthy for churches to disagree? What are some healthy ways individuals within a church can disagree and still be unified? On what differences might it actually be healthy for individuals in a church to part ways?

5. Define and describe the necessary components of conflict resolution.

6. On a scale of 1–10, where 10 represents the greatest level of health, where would you say your church is right now in the discipline of consistently working through its conflicts?

7. What is one action you can take this week to promote or restore greater unity in your church?

Spend some time praying about relationships in your church. Ask God to strengthen and bless them. Ask God for help in mending torn or broken relationships.

Trait 6: An Irresistible Church Is Always Learning

Remember the Big Idea

As churches, we tend to favor stability over change. Often our greatest unspoken goal is to arrive at a good place and then stay put. But an irresistible church chooses to constantly learn and adapt. Change is the currency of a constantly shifting society, and what worked yesterday to minister to that society may not always work today.

An irresistible church does not change for change's sake alone. The main emphasis is never placed on being relevant, current, or "cool." Rather, we must choose to change because God uses the agent of change for His good. God knows that once people stop learning new things they stop growing. The human spirit thrives on learning about God, His will, others, and oneself. Sometimes change is necessary in order to reach new groups of people.

Study God's Word

1. Read Proverbs 14:4 (NLT), then discuss the thought, "If our goal is a clean manger, we won't have any strength or effectiveness."

2. Why is it dangerous for a church to change for the sake of change alone? Is it ever possible to change too much, too quickly, or for the wrong reasons?

3. On a scale of 1–10, the greatest level of health being a 10, where would you say your church is now in its commitment to constant learning?

4. What's the difference between discussion and argument? How can you ensure that an evaluation meeting involves discussion without arguments?

5. Read Exodus 18:5–27. In this story, how was Moses well-meaning but ineffectual in his leadership, and how did his father-in-law help him change for the better?

6. In what areas of your life or your church can you apply the story you just read? In other words, are there any areas of service where you are well-meaning or well-entrenched, yet ineffectual? What changes need to occur?

7. What is one action you can take this week toward learning something new?

Spend some time praying that God would help you and your church change in response to His call on your life to transform into His likeness, as well as to help disciple others.

Trait 7: An Irresistible Church Promotes Spiritual Self-Feeding

Remember the Big Idea

An irresistible church is filled with self-feeders. Feeding ourselves spiritually is no one else's responsibility but our own. I cannot expect others to feed me. If I am to grow and mature, it is not the responsibility of a pastor or an elder or a Sunday school teacher. Certainly these people will help coach me, instruct me, encourage me, and sharpen my skills; but I alone am responsible for feeding myself.

Study God's Word

1. How does Psalm 46:10 encourage us to be a self-feeder? How would you apply this to everyday life?

2. Name some typical barriers to self-feeding. Why do some people find it difficult to regularly read the Bible, pray, and spend time alone with God?

3. Read Psalm 119:32–35. In this passage, what benefit to following Christ is described? What are some practical ways we can run in the path of God's commands? What does it look like when Christ sets our heart free?

4. Read Hebrews 4:12. How is the Bible alive?

5. Read Psalm 16:8. According to this verse, what is our responsibility, and what is the benefit?

6. What might it look like to arrive at church already motivated to grow? What helps motivate us in this area?

7. In what ways are you already a spiritual self-feeder? How can you better yourself in this area?

Spend some time praying, thanking God for His Word, and asking for His help in being a spiritual self-feeder.

Trait 8: An Irresistible Church Connects Everything to a Soul

Remember the Big Idea

An irresistible church connects everything it does to a soul. That means every function of the church is connected to the mission of saving the lost and helping people grow in the faith. A church is not simply a social club or a community of people who rally around a common cause. There's earnestness and purposefulness to our work because of the eternal consequences. God invites us to love, serve, and obey Him, and part of the adventure of following Him means that we get to have a hand in helping people find their way to the Lord.

Study God's Word

1. Read Revelation 21–22:5. List some of the descriptions of the new heaven and earth found in this passage. What do you look forward to most?

2. Read Matthew 22:34–40. What are the two greatest commandments?

3. Read Matthew 28:18–20. What does Jesus tell His disciples to do?

4. How should all functions of a church relate in some way to Matthew 22:34–40 and Matthew 28:18–20? Give some examples.

5. To what degree would you say everything in your church is connected to its mission? Do you get the sense that people know the true function of a church and live that way?

6. What does it mean that we help lead people to Christ together? In your own life, how satisfied are you with the number of people you have helped lead to Christ?

7. Do some creative brainstorming. List three or four functions of your church, and then tell how each connects back to a soul. (Some examples might include the work of the administrative assistant; custodial work; special gifts toward special departments, such as youth ministry; motorcycle ministry; recovery ministry.)

8. How might you connect to a soul what you personally do at your church or during the week outside the church?

Trait 9: An Irresistible Church Chooses to Love

Remember the Big Idea

An irresistible church loves the people in her community as well as her call to reach them. The greatest love is a love of choice. The Bible calls this kind of love *agape*.

Many factors exist that can motivate a person to serve Christ, yet some other motivations (such as guilt) succeed mostly in burning a person out or in creating a false sense of duty. Second Corinthians 5:14 shows us a better way: "Christ's love compels us." The concept is both freeing and empowering. When we love someone deeply we serve with a glad heart. Our actions are characterized by a sustainable passion—one that does not flare up nor die down quickly.

Study God's Word

1. Discuss the various motives people or churches can have for serving God. Then read 2 Corinthians 5:14. How can our love for God be the best motivation for service?

2. Read Matthew 20:30–34. How does Christ's example of compassion motivate us to serve others?

3. To what degree would you say love for God and love for people guide the various functions of your church?

4. Choose a specific ministry in your church that is functioning well, and trace the connection between that ministry and love. For instance: *We can see that people in our church genuinely love high school students because they are more than willing to go on retreats with them and do the work necessary to make the retreat successful.*

5. We find time to do the things we love to do. How can you see this principle at work in your own life?

6. Read Exodus 4:1–17. What is Moses' attitude toward service as we see exhibited in this passage? What's the connection between serving God out of love and serving God out of obedience?

7. How does the action of praying for a person or region before ministering to them help to develop love for that person or region?

Spend some time praying for the people in your church and community. Ask the Lord to give you a strong love and compassion for these people.

Trait 10: An Irresistible Church Takes Risks

Remember the Big Idea

An irresistible church takes risks. A risk, in this sense, is when a church steps forward in faith to minister in new kingdom-building initiatives. She responds in obedience to the leading of God.

Like a toddler taking her first steps, if a church does not choose to risk, a church will not grow. When we purposely disturb our comfort and stability for the sake of advancing the kingdom, spiritual growth occurs. A church that takes risks is a church that understands faith is alive. Our calling is not to arrive at a destination of stability, but to travel a pathway of constant growth and transformation. In order to live by faith, we must be willing to disturb the equilibrium of our lives.

Study God's Word

1. How can stability and comfort become death sentences for a church?

2. "Risk is not haphazard, but based on God's guidance." Explain.

3. On a scale of 1–10, with 10 being the most risky, to what degree is your church a risk-taking church?

4. What truths are learned from 1 John 4:15 and John 16:13 and how might these truths apply to our churches' taking risks?

5. In what ways does the truth of Romans 8:28 factor into God's guidance?

6. Have you ever experienced a situation where you took a risk for the Lord and it didn't turn out as you'd hoped? What happened? Has your perspective on the situation changed?

7. Read Mark 4:1–20. According to this passage, how much failure can be expected when we scatter spiritual seed? According to verse 20, how much success will result? What has been your experience with scattering spiritual seed?

8. In what new areas of growth do you see your church being obedient to God?

Trait 11: An Irresistible Church Humbles Itself

Remember the Big Idea

The eleventh trait of an irresistible church is humility. This characteristic is demonstrated when a church follows the teaching found in James 4:10 and humbles itself so the Lord can lift it up in due time. This teaching is also found in 1 Peter 5:5–6: "God opposes the proud, but gives grace to the humble. Humble yourselves, therefore, under God's mighty hand, that he may lift you up in due time."

Humility is remembering who we are in light of who God is. As Christians, we have a vital assignment that we don't want to miss. It's easy to get caught up in many things and miss what we're supposed to be about. But we are called to serve God and called to pour our lives into significant matters. Sometimes what is significant can look different than what we expect. Matthew 10:42 says that even a cup of cold water given to one of the least of Christ's followers will not go unrewarded. Our invitation is to represent and radiate Christ, to be an ambassador for Him, to think what He thinks, and to speak what He speaks. Our calling is to serve God in any way He asks us to.

Study God's Word

1. Read James 4:10 and 1 Peter 5:5–6. What does it look like for a church to humble itself? How might the Lord lift that church up?

2. On a scale of 1–10, with 10 being humble and 1 being proud, where would you say your church stands?

3. Read Matthew 6:1–18. With what posture of the heart does the Bible tell us to pray, give to the needy, and fast?

4. Read Matthew 5:16. What is the balance between letting

your light shine before men and doing good deeds in secret or anonymously?

5. What is one step you could take this week to do a hidden act of kindness?

6. How can intentionally thinking through your church's mission be an act of humility?

7. Read 1 Samuel 31 and 2 Samuel 1:1–15. What mistake did the young Amalekite make, and what lessons can we learn from this story? Give some practical examples of what this might look like in everyday life.

Spend some time in prayer, asking the Lord to show you any areas of unconfessed pride. In prayer, resolve to humble yourself and allow the Lord to lift you up in due time.

Trait 12: An Irresistible Church Has a Plan

Remember the Big Idea

The twelfth trait of an irresistible church is that it has a plan. This kind of church has earnestly sought God's guidance, developed a blueprint from that guidance, and then boldly stepped forward to implement the plan.

Study God's Word

1. Read James 4:13–15. What important attitude of the heart is necessary when making our plans?

2. Read Proverbs 16:1, 9; 19:21; and 20:24, then Proverbs 16:3; 20:18; and Psalm 20:4. What do these passages teach us about making plans?

3. To what degree would you say your church currently has a plan? Are people aware of that plan, and are they acting on it?

4. Read Matthew 6:22–23. How can adopting a biblically positive outlook on life help us live with victory, strength, and confidence?

5. When you imagine your church's preferred future, what does your church look like? You may want to develop a list of various areas and ministries within the church.

6. Read Psalm 8:1 and 2 Corinthians 3:18. If God's name depicts His character, then what kind of God do we serve? If we are being transformed into His likeness, what might we look like as we become people—and churches—of excellence?

7. Read 1 Chronicles 12:32. How can your church become like the men of Issachar, who "understood the times and knew what [they] should do"? List some practical steps your church can take.

Spend some time in prayer, asking the Lord what His plan for your church is. Then ask Him for the strength to take action on that plan.

NOTES

TRAIT 1: Hungers for the Presence of God

1. See William Jennings Bryan (editor-in-chief), Francis W. Halsey (associate editor), *The World's Famous Orations, Vol. IX* (New York: Funk and Wagnalls).
2. As quoted in Randy C. Alcorn, *The Law of Rewards: Giving What You Can't Keep to Gain What You Can't Lose* (Carol Stream, IL: Tyndale House, 2003), 18.

TRAIT 3: Lives Heart First

1. "1 Song, but 2 Girls," Sky Canaves and Geoffrey Fowler, *The Wall Street Journal*, August 13, 2008, *http://online.wsj.com/article/SB121859320884635553.html*. Accessed July 2010.
2. For an in-depth examination of the biblical process of forgiveness, I recommend R. T. Kendall's *Total Forgiveness* (Lake Mary, FL: Charisma House, 2007).

TRAIT 4: Practices Gratefulness

1. See Rabbi Noah Weinberg, *The 5 Levels of Pleasure* (New York: Select Books, 2008).

TRAIT 5: Promotes Healthy Relationships

1. See Mother Teresa, *Mother Teresa: In My Own Words* (New York: Gramercy Books, a division of Random House Value Publishing, 1977).

TRAIT 6: Is Always Learning

1. See Anne Blunt and Wilfrid Scawen Blunt, *Bedouin Tribes of the Euphrates* (New York: Harper, 1879).
2. See Alvin Toffler, *The Third Wave* (New York: Random House, 1987).
3. See Martin Luther, John Dillenberger, ed., *Martin Luther: Selections From His Writings* (New York: Doubleday, 1962).
4. See Mark Twain, *Mark Twain: Collected Tales, Sketches, Speeches, and Essays, Volume. 2: 1891–1910* (New York: Library of America, Penguin Putnam Inc., 1992).

TRAIT 7: Promotes Spiritual Self-Feeding

1. *The American Journal of Medicine* (New York: Thomson Reuters).

TRAIT 8: Connects Everything to a Soul

1. Eliza E. Hewitt, "When We All Get to Heaven" (public domain, 1898).
2. Theodore O. Wedel, "Evangelism—the Mission of the Church to Those Outside Her Life," *The Ecumenical Review,* October 1953, 24.

TRAIT 11: Humbles Itself

1. Name has been changed.

TRAIT 12: Has a Plan

1. *http://disneyparks.disney.go.com/blog/2010/05/a-moment-with-art/.* Accessed August 2010.

ACKNOWLEDGMENTS

I t is an understatement to say how much I appreciate all the people it takes to be an irresistible church.

I especially appreciate those who assist me (and are much smarter than I am in everything): Mary Waialeale for her faithful assistance; Elwin Ahu for leading so well as I focus on the colleges we oversee; John Tilton for your oversight; and the many other leaders who have been raised up. I am always humbled by your commitment.

I am also thankful for my editing team of Marcus Brotherton and Ellen Chalifoux. Scattered thoughts go in one end and literary prose comes out the other. You make me look much better than I really am.

Thanks to Kyle Duncan and the excellent team at Bethany House Publishers, and especially my agent Greg Johnson at the WordServe Literary Group.

Our church council has been more than partners. They have become friends along the way: Greg Kemp, Murray Hohns, Glenn Ogasawara, Robert Miura, Phil Suh, Ken Souza, Dayne Kaneshiro, and Dave Sorensen. When I wrestled with my health, they were like Aaron and Hur alongside of Moses, holding up his hands until victory was achieved. And now as my seasons change and I am working on training leaders, these saints continue to support not only the present but the future of our great church. You are the very kind of people who help make for an irresistible church.

WAYNE CORDEIRO is senior pastor of New Hope Christian Fellowship in Oahu, Hawaii, which is listed as one of the top twenty-five most influential churches and one of the top ten most innovative churches in America.

Wayne is a church planter at heart and has been instrumental in planting more than a hundred churches in the Pacific Rim countries of the Philippines, Japan, Australia, and Myanmar, as well as in Hawaii, California, Montana, Washington, and Nevada. At last count, more than eighty-three thousand people have made first-time decisions for Christ through these churches.

In addition to his responsibilities at New Hope Oahu, Wayne has recently accepted the role of president of his alma mater, Eugene Bible College, now known as New Hope Christian College. NHCC is now part of a consortium of Pacific Rim Christian Colleges with locations in Hawaii, Oregon, Myanmar, and Tokyo.

Wayne has authored ten books, including *Doing Church as a Team, Dream Releasers, The Seven Rules of Success, Culture Shift, Attitudes That Attract Success, The Divine Mentor,* and *Leading On Empty.* Wayne is also the author of the *Life Journal,* which is being used by thousands of churches worldwide in bringing people back to the Word of God.

Wayne and his wife, Anna, have been married for more than thirty-five years. They have three married children and four grandchildren. Wayne's hobbies include music, reading, water sports, riding his Harley-Davidson, and training horses. Wayne and Anna now split their time between Hawaii and Eugene, Oregon, where they have a family farm.

A Lifeline for Leaders

The pressure, stress, and overwhelming demands of a life of ministry leave leaders feeling burned out. Sharing from his own experiences, Wayne Cordeiro shows how to avoid burnout and renew a fruitful, balanced, and healthy ministry and life.

Leading on Empty

"This is a must-read for all leaders."
—Bill Hybels,
Senior Pastor, Willow Creek Community Church

Revive Your Quiet Time

Discover how to enjoy a dynamic, vital, and intimate relationship with God—it may just save your health, your marriage, your ministry, and your future.

The Divine Mentor

"Wayne Cordeiro's message and ministry are a gift to the kingdom of God. I'm confident his book will be an encouragement to all who read it."
—Max Lucado, bestselling author